PRAISE FOR
THE CONTEMPLATIVE LEADER

"Such a generous and skillful offering! If you want to use your power and influence for good in this world, here is your practice manual. May you have the discipline and commitment to use it well."

—Margaret J. Wheatley, Bestselling Author, *Leadership and the New Science* and *Who Do We Choose to Be?*

"This groundbreaking book gives a compelling vision for those who want to lead from a deeper place. More than just another book on tools and tips for those in positions of responsibility, it is a call to cultivate a depth of spirit, a care of soul, and a servant mindset. It reminds us transformational leadership flows not from titles or positions but on those who carry themselves with an inner authority that bears fruit in an authentic, loving, and generative life."

—Daniel G. Groody, Vice President and Associate Provost for Undergraduate Education, Professor of Theology and Global Affairs, University of Notre Dame

"*The Contemplative Leader* is timely in a constantly changing world; who we are and how we lead is more critical than ever. Patrick's challenge to his readers to find the space to be their integrated selves—the goal of contemplation—is refreshing and speaks to the desire of people to be led by leaders who are authentic. From start to finish, he takes you through both ancient wisdom and the latest psychological theories in an insightful, practical, and a deeply engaging way. This book has the potential to re-define what it means to lead in the modern era."

—Tom Hall, Global Head of Social Impact, UBS, and former Head of Bank of Ireland Asset Management, Ireland

"In *The Contemplative Leader*, Patrick generously guides leaders of all types away from rigid and brittle tactics and toward a more natural and heartfelt style where ideas and creativity can be shared in an effortless flow. It's pretty amazing. Somehow he's managed to put his intelligence into book form and, seeing as he's both brilliant and deeply charming, this is no small feat."

—Pete Holmes, Comedian, Writer, and Podcast
Host, *You Made It Weird with Pete Holmes*

"This exquisitely researched and written book is a must-read for everyone who aspires to stand up and lead. Harnessing ancient wisdom and cutting-edge science, it is a powerful and practical invitation to bring positive possibility to every moment through harnessing presence, purpose, and a deep connection to the both/and of the whole self."

—Louise Chester, Founder, Mindfulness at Work and Purpose at Work,
and Global Ambassador, Center for Compassionate Leadership

"Learning to see what's 'really real' is a lost art, and Patrick Boland is one of the most trustworthy guides I know. In *The Contemplative Leader*, he invites truly radical shifts of perspective and practice. This book is for leaders of all kinds who know that our work isn't about us at all, and who want to lead and be led toward matters more vital than mere success or failure."

—Michael Poffenberger, Executive Director,
Center for Action and Contemplation

"As revolution in leadership goes on, this book is a must-read for all leaders who would like to bring their authentic selves to leadership, who both care for and embrace their people, who care for both the means and the ends, who believe meaning and purpose can be found and lived through leadership."

—Gulru Atak, Transaction Banking Head of Europe, Barclays

"This book is a gift. The experience of reading Patrick's book will stay with you. It opens up possibilities to personally reflect, to look at experiences through different lenses; and, to create fresh thinking about leadership presence. Patrick skillfully explains models in a way that is accessible and insightful. There is so much in this book that will inform the thinking, growth; and impact of leaders—at every stage—as they make progress."

—Hannah Carney, Executive Coach, former Lawyer, and Time to Think™ Coach and Facilitator

"With his book *The Contemplative Leader*, Patrick Boland has created something very special and unique. It is a tour de force spanning both wide scholarship and practical deep exercises. Patrick also makes authentic use of his own journey of contemplation, growth, challenges, and learning. I have no hesitation in strongly recommending this book."

—Tom Finlay, Coach, Coach Supervisor, Therapist, Poet, Independent Director, and Coauthor, *Deep Joy: Reflections on Life.*

"The really great leaders in life are those who readily connect with people. This book should be on the desk of every leader who is aiming to bring their leadership and connection skills to a new level of excellence."

—Helen Dooley, Group General Counsel, AIB Bank, Ireland

"This book gleaned from a contemplative mind is most definitely a departure from the plethora of books on leadership. Patrick Boland demonstrates how contemplation enables us to come home and be present to ourselves and be present and connected with others in a very deep way. It demonstrates that when we are centered and connected, we can think more clearly and creatively and lead authentically. Through contemplation, we become more grounded and more aware and feel more connected to the world around us. Moving from a place of stillness we are more capable of having right understanding and taking right action. *The Contemplative Leader* teaches us to look directly at what authentic leadership is, with clarity and without judgement, and invites us to enter a process to get there. This is a very powerful and empowering book that has the potential to change lives."

—Sr. Stanislaus Kennedy, Founder, FOCUS Ireland and The Sanctuary

"I wholeheartedly recommend *The Contemplative Leader* by Patrick Boland. Having worked closely with him, I have personally witnessed his passion and exceptional ability to guide people towards a profound understanding of wholeness. Patrick's brilliance lies in his skillful translation of wisdom tools into practical and impactful resources for leaders seeking meaning and growth. This insightful and engaging book is a testament to Patrick's years of research and his extensive experience coaching and inspiring world-class leaders to evolve in their roles. If you're looking to elevate your leadership and embrace a contemplative approach, *The Contemplative Leader* is the perfect guide for you."

—Kirsten Oates, Cohost, *Turning to the Mystics* Podcast

"To many people, 'contemplative' and 'leader' might seem like opposites. But read Patrick Boland and discover why this is not true—and need not be true for you or your organization."

—Fr. Richard Rohr O.F.M., Founder, Center
for Action and Contemplation

THE

CONTEMPLATIVE

LEADER

ALSO BY PATRICK BOLAND

Every Thing Is Sacred (coauthored with Richard Rohr)

THE

CONTEMPLATIVE

LEADER

Uncover the Power of
Presence and Connection

PATRICK BOLAND

Matt Holt Books
An Imprint of BenBella Books, Inc.
Dallas, TX

Matt Holt is an imprint of BenBella Books, Inc.
10440 N. Central Expressway
Suite 800
Dallas, TX 75231
benbellabooks.com
Send feedback to feedback@benbellabooks.com

BenBella and *Matt Holt* are federally registered trademarks.

Printed in the United States of America
10 9 8 7 6 5 4 3 2 1

Library of Congress Control Number: 2023025220
ISBN 9781637744277 (hardcover)
ISBN 9781637744284 (electronic)

Editing by Katie Dickman
Copyediting by Lydia Choi
Proofreading by Ashley Casteel and Jenny Bridges
Indexing by WordCo Indexing Services, Inc.
Text design and composition by Aaron Edmiston
Graphic diagrams by Lucy Kelly, Lucinda Grace Design
Cover design by Brigid Pearson
Cover image © Shutterstock / SantaLiza
Printed by Lake Book Manufacturing

Special discounts for bulk sales are available.
Please contact bulkorders@benbellabooks.com.

For Patrick Luca

CONTENTS

Part I: The Inner Journey of Contemplative Leadership

Part II: The Outer Journey of Contemplative Leadership

FOREWORD

The word "contemplative" is still vaguely defined in most of our minds. It was repopularized in our times by the American Trappist monk Thomas Merton in the 1960s. He used it very positively and constantly but largely without ever precisely defining it. Yet it worked his magic. The very word "contemplation" still makes many of us jump to a strange attention, as if our deeper consciousness knows, "There is something important here!"

Patrick Boland is one of those people who has jumped to attention. He enjoys a rare combination of gifts and education, executive coaching, and years of serious interest in the contemplative mind and practice. The excellent result is this book. It is a well-integrated book that invites you, the reader, to join him in the jump! By integrated, I mean he has put many disciplines together in a way that feeds body, mind, soul, and spirit all at the same time. He could only write in such a way if he had first put the same together within himself. Then it is like breathing.

In this book you will find intelligence, developmental and leadership theories, psychological insight, poetry, and spirituality all assaulting you on the same page. You are being led. And that is what contemplative leaders cannot *not* do! They lead largely by their presence and their vital energy—much more than with their words.

So, they are doing it all the time, even when you do not expect it—and they are not trying. They do not need a declared role or title, but they still lead you by the way they are with you and with others.

If this is so, there must be non-contemplative leaders, too. People who push you around, merely entertain you, or poison you while you strangely ask for more. Perhaps this explains a bit of why so many countries continue to elect utterly unqualified human beings to high office. Like is attracted to like, I guess. If you have done no inner work, you will applaud people who are just like you. You have to have a bit of contemplative quiet in you to even pick up a book like this. So, trust yourself and keep reading. You are jumping to attention now. And you have a good guide here.

Let's try this for an attempt at a description of contemplation. Even the Latin and English roots of the word imply looking or seeing—how you look and how you see the moment. In my own observation and lifetime of leading groups and retreat work, I have recognized at least three common ways that most people look at their world. I call them *glaring, glancing,* and *gazing.* Not only is beauty in the eye of the beholder; just about everything else is, too.

> **Glaring:** Looking with suspicion, judgment, and negation as the first lens.
>
> **Glancing:** A normal default position; quick looking around; unconsciousness.
>
> **Gazing:** A long, loving look at anything. Seeing that morphs into appreciation.

All three of them are learned and practiced, and until you recognize your practical addiction to one of them, you will not move toward another. *Glaring* is learned by hurts and aggressions, sometimes even trauma, and it lives in the body even more than in the mind. So glarers usually cannot be *talked* out of their state. Notice how wounded leaders seem so unreasonable, even operating against their own happiness and freedom. They are usually fear based, and they call their fear "reality." They must feel safe and loved *in their body*, or glarers will not change or grow.

Glancing is living on the surface of your own life. It comes naturally to leaders who have never learned from love and suffering, which are the master teachers. Glancing is really not seeing at all but merely skimming the surface and retaining yourself as the central reference point. It is *my* feelings, *my* hurts, *my* fears, and *my* opinions that alone keep them alive. Their frame of reference is thus very small. Glancing leaders tend not to talk about ideas or events but only about people—and how people affect them. And, forgive me, but nobody really cares except other glancers. Their blind spot, as M. Scott Peck says in *The Road Less Traveled*, is basically laziness and lack of curiosity about the world, creation, and even themselves. They lack soul. They also must learn from the master teachers of love and suffering, or they will never discover their own depths nor have any interest in others' depths.

Gazing is a chosen, conscious state—even though you "fall into it" more than you consciously choose it, which at first sounds like a contradiction. It is precisely not *self*-consciousness except insofar as I recognize that I am the Seer here and my biases and blockages are always getting in the way. Gazing approaches pure consciousness—where I as the looker and the objects I am looking at move into the background. The art and act of *appreciation* itself takes over, and any depreciation seems almost impossible except by accident. Thus, it becomes the very act of loving. The contemplative leader can readily see the shadow, the broken side of everything, but the contemplative leader is not only fully motivated to "forgive" any imperfection but also to even include all shadow material inside of its overwhelming light, not by killing it but by absorbing it. This is how light overcomes darkness.

Artists and poets are often the first to realize this state (it is a state), but so are many musicians and scientists, at least indirectly. I wish I could put clergy as commonly in this state, but we tend to be trained in making dualistic judgments instead, which keeps us glaring far too much.

Merton called those who gaze "masked contemplatives." They are everywhere, in all cultures and religions, many not formally religious at all, and all they need is a more mature contemplative leader to model the way. It is a maturing process that never stops maturing. Let's first look for *contemplative* leaders to lead us; age, nationality, religion, and formal education are much further down the list. Gazing might just be the most simple form of connection there is. Just stay with a long, loving look at just about anything until it turns *you* into the good, the true, and the beautiful. If you don't get waylaid by negative glaring and mere glancing, I promise you it will.

Patrick Boland is showing you in this book how to lead yourself and, maybe more importantly, who is worth following.

Richard Rohr, OFM
Center for Action and Contemplation
Albuquerque, New Mexico

INTRODUCTION

At the still point of the turning world . . .
Where past and future are gathered. Neither
*   movement from nor towards,*
Neither ascent nor decline. Except for the point, the
*   still point,*
There would be no dance, and there is only the dance.
—T. S. Eliot, *Burnt Norton*[1]

THE INTERCONNECTIONS
OF LEADERSHIP

Whether we formally occupy a position of leadership in an organization or we simply interact with colleagues, friends, and family, every one of us influences the lives of those around us in ways that previous generations could not have imagined. From global video calls to trending social media platforms, we are leading and influencing more people than most of us realize. Political movements grow exponentially when one video goes viral. Influencers' posts can add or subtract millions, even billions, to or from the value of a company in a matter of hours. The long-term, steady growth of traditional organizations can be undone by the disruptive innovation of market

1

entrants in just a few years, even months. New organizations have flatter structures than ever before, with younger generations expecting to have access to senior leaders and for their insights to be acted upon. Seasoned leaders who have risen to roles of positional leadership over many years are faced with competing, ever-changing external pressures that are out of their control.

In this rapidly evolving environment, we are tempted to react, to fix, to problem-solve—to try anything that will give us some sense of stability. But the interconnection of these unpredictable and evolving relational, economic, and political forces means that we will never "be in control." It doesn't matter what title we have or how much experience we have with leading within a closed, predictable system. Our ability to effectively lead is now less dependent on any formal position that we hold and much more dependent on our capacity to engage with people and evolving systems from a place of inner poise. But cultivating this inner poise, what I call *contemplative presence*, can be very challenging in the busy environment of everyday leadership.

The Irish phrase *grinn aithint* beautifully proposes the antidote. It describes people who have "awareness with discernment," an ability to see "through the superficial and the surface to the core essence of someone or something." They are able to recognize "the true nature of an object, an event, or a person."[2] But how do we develop this capacity to see the essence of what's happening with people within our organization in the wider global context of our leadership? To go outside ourselves and lead others requires us first to go within. This book will cover how to develop as a contemplative leader who embodies a deeply rooted presence and has a capacity to meaningfully connect with others as we lead.

PRESENCE AND CONNECTION: FROM EDUCATORS TO EXECUTIVES

My experience of contemplative leaders began with some teachers I had in school. The most memorable of them had two key characteristics in common: a sense of personal presence about them and an ability to connect with others. The teachers who did a really great job, whom we still remember for all the right reasons, were comfortable being themselves. A few were quirky or funny, some were sharp, and others were strict—but what they all had in common was a high degree of self-acceptance, which translated as an ease in how they showed up. They were authentically themselves. And although they were often quite aware of what we thought of them, our opinions weren't the main driver influencing their behaviors.

But even though many teachers had a strong sense of presence, few were able to translate this into communicating their message and getting us to follow along. Only those who could meet us where *we* were at, who could really connect with us, earned our respect and our buy-in. By communicating a real interest in us and in our world, they successfully inspired us to take responsibility for our own learning.

Teachers of this kind used a variety of styles and approaches with different students. From asking us incisive questions to occasionally sharing personal stories, referring to famous examples or referencing pop culture, they had a way of piquing our interest to the point that we became personally invested in knowing more. They influenced us to engage in topics in ways we hadn't previously imagined. And when we became stuck or disinterested, it was our respect for them that kept us focused. Their presence and personal connection inspired us to dig deeper and continue along our own path of development.

Originally, I supposed this dynamic only applied to great teachers. But as I started my career, I observed this same "presence and connection" factor across all my experiences of excellent leadership. From sports coaching to banking, tech firms to the nonprofit sector, spiritual leadership to the fast-moving consumer goods industry, the most effective leaders within each type of organization have an ability to connect with others from a place of authentic presence. Amidst the accelerating pace of Eliot's "turning world," these leaders focus on "the still point" of *this* moment. Aware that here is "where past and future are gathered," they honor the past and prepare for the future by fully engaging with *who* and *what* they experience in the here and now.

Presence is what great leaders have and connection is what they do.

Whether they get paid for it or not, whether they lead a large team of executives or work as an individual contributor, those who influence and lead with great resonance delve deeply into the source of their own presence in ways that allow them to meaningfully connect with those around them.

I went on to pursue the twin tracks of performance-based and presence-based leadership: I studied international commerce while also leading men's groups; I worked as a strategy consultant and then completed a master's degree in counseling and trained as a psychotherapist; I worked as an executive coach and leadership consultant while also running retreats and Mindfulness programs. These two paths of engaging with contemplative traditions while also working with leaders seemed to weave their way into my life. As I made my way in my career journey, I continued to ask: How can we lead from a place of depth and authenticity while also pursuing excellence and meaningful impact? Across all my diverse experiences, I found these various fields used different language to explain similar concepts of leadership based on presence and connection. I became fascinated with the inspiration behind and essence of our leadership, wondering:

- Why do certain situations inspire us to speak up and actively contribute?
- What does this say about who we are?
- How do we seek to lead and influence as a result?

INFLUENCING WITH PRESENCE

When I was sixteen, I asked my parents for a copy of Niccolò Machiavelli's classic Renaissance-era book *The Prince* as my Christmas present. It might seem strange, but I'd just read an excerpt in history class, and it had sounded like perfect reading for any young person looking to make their way in the world. There's a lot of pragmatic wisdom in *The Prince*, all focused on achieving significant leadership goals. However, as the critics of its time so succinctly put it, one key message of the book is that, when it comes to leadership, "the ends justify the means." Although it is now often regarded as an outdated manual for acquiring and maintaining power, some of the utilitarian conclusions that Machiavelli draws are very similar to how outcome-oriented leaders rationalize their achievements today.

We can easily forget that the way we participate in everything we do communicates the kind of leader we are. This greatly impacts the way we show up in every interaction, impacting the quality of our presence in each meeting and our ability to authentically connect with, and influence, the wider organizational context. When our focus is on achieving big results, we can become too task-focused to consider the means we are using to get things done. We need to find ways to focus on both the means *and* the ends. This is where a contemplative approach to leadership is most valuable.

Reframing the concept of leadership as our ability to influence others is a helpful first step in actively taking responsibility for what we do and how we do it. When our external world is ever-changing, we need to go inside to our internal world and connect with what is most valuable, meaningful, and true of ourselves. It's only as we do this that we build a solid foundation on which to base the *why* and the *how* of our leadership.

We can only lead others as far as we have first gone ourselves.

From my experience coaching leaders in a variety of global organizations, as well as my work as a psychotherapist, it's clear to me that we can only meaningfully engage with others to the extent that we have already engaged with ourselves. Our capacity to lead others is based on the overflow of our own sense of presence and inner connection. This book focuses on this most foundational aspect to leadership, exploring the various components of our presence, connecting and reconnecting us with the essence of who we are.

No matter how much we know about our organization, our people, and our own capabilities and leadership, the uncertainties of tomorrow and the complexities of our contexts and relationships today all invite us beyond a tips-and-techniques approach to leading. We need to practice holding the tension between influencing from a place of authenticity and accepting that we cannot *fully* control any situation or outcome. Contemplation helps us look out on the world with a humble attitude of accepting that we are not fully in control; that we will never have *all* the relevant data to make a decision or know *exactly* what to do in every situation; that there will always be more to see, to learn, and to experience in our lived moments of leadership. But instead of growing despondent at this awareness, we can instead use contemplation to help us focus our attention on our lived experiences in *this* moment.

Leading in a contemplative way is both process oriented and outcome oriented. It endows us with a humble confidence that awakens and opens us to experiencing what *is* happening rather than simply projecting our own version of reality into every situation we face. We can listen to others because we have first listened to ourselves. Sitting with the challenges that have shaped us, far from something negative, teaches us to notice when we are spurred to act out of scarcity and fear. This helps us become aware of our deeper motivations for building, overcoming, and achieving "great goals." Contemplative leaders notice the energetic difference between doing something just to feel good about themselves and acting from a place of inner conviction. They don't *need* to lead anything. Power, position, and proving oneself are not that important to them. What is most important is how they bring their energies into the causes that compel them to lead.

No matter how much we long for it to be the case, most real-world leadership challenges don't have simple solutions. They require a nuanced kind of processing on our part. And this is where non-dualistic ways of thinking and seeing come in:

- I can be friendly with my colleagues *and* have clear boundaries with them around work.
- I can stand behind my actions *and* know that the board members may not be happy with the decisions I have made.
- I can recommend that we proceed with this merger *and* accept that I cannot totally control how things will pan out in five years' time.

As we learn and practice non-dualistic thinking, we become less attached to controlling outcomes to go exactly our way. This "letting go" frees us to experience the kind of change and evolution that is fundamental to all organisms and systems. When we let go of some of our assumptions about leadership, we allow ourselves to experience the situations we face without a list of preconceived ideas of "how things should be." The goal of dualistic thinking is to feel in control, but the goal of non-dualistic, nonattached thinking is to be open to what unfolds as a result of our participation and best efforts, which, paradoxically, creates the conditions for even greater things to happen than what we could have planned. The paradoxical theory of change tells us that it is only when we stop trying to control how and when change takes place that we allow the conditions for change to occur.[3]

Contemplative leadership trusts that great outcomes follow great processes, so once an overarching strategy is in place, it then turns its attention to focusing on the process. It is this "both/and" way of thinking about things that makes contemplative leadership different. It focuses on, for example:

- *Both* the financials *and* the people
- *Both* the results *and* the road that gets us there
- *Both* the personal benefits to me *and* the impact on the wider organization and community

When we lead from this contemplative standpoint of nonattachment, we become comfortable embracing paradox, sitting with the tension of not always knowing how things will play out. Tempting as it is to seek more and more control in the face of uncertainty, contemplative leaders instead focus on being present to themselves, listening to others, and connecting with their environment.

BECOMING A CONTEMPLATIVE LEADER

The regular practice of self-examination, combined with embodied exercises of contemplation, allows us to return to a fundamental groundedness—a foundational presence from which our everyday leadership influence emanates. To journey toward this foundational source, we need to explore the inner workings of our interior world. Borrowing the language of Thomas Merton, this interior world is made up of our False Self and our True Self.[4] The False Self is who we think we are, who society has told us we need to be. This includes roles such as "parent," titles such as "Senior Vice President," and identities such as "I'm a results-oriented leader." None of these examples has to be inaccurate, *per se*, but if we overidentify with these labels, we don't get to connect with or lead from our True Self.

Our True Self is who we are at our core. As some Zen Buddhist masters teach, it is "the face you had before you were born." When we remove all our masks, the noise of the roles, titles, and identities that have served to develop us as leaders in the world, then what is left is our True Self. It's always been there. It's the part of us that philosophy and religion often call the soul.[5] I like to refer to the combination

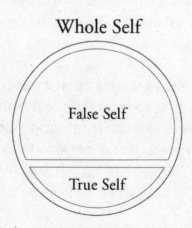

Whole Self

False Self

True Self

of our False and True Selves as our Whole Self, as this term is broad enough to encompass our conscious and unconscious awareness, facets of ourselves we are comfortable with as well as facets we struggle to see or accept. There is a place for all these facets in our Whole Self. It's not that the False Self is "bad" and the True Self is "good"; they both play an important role in how we show up in daily life.

We are always leading and influencing from this Whole Self. We often lead from our False Self with its roles and titles, self-importance, and need to be right, but every now and then we catch a glimpse of our True Self peeping through. We remove the mask and accept the person, the situation, ourselves. And we sense an authority that comes from deep within, a presence that connects with others.

As we uncover more of our Whole Self, we come to deeply embody our values and evolving motivations across the span of our life. We acknowledge the different masks we wear in various scenarios and accept that there's a place for each of them. We very slowly come to see the shadow that we carry, the parts of us that everyone else sees that we struggle to recognize or accept. We become aware of how this shadow sometimes adversely affects the ways we interact with and influence others, and we can take steps to alleviate its more challenging side effects. Our convictions deepen, our ability to influence develops, and the teams, organizations, and communities that we help shape can thrive.

Over time, as we dedicate ourselves to exploring and taking responsibility for our Whole Self, our internal world becomes mirrored in our external world.

HOW TO APPROACH THIS BOOK

*Until you make the unconscious conscious, it will
direct your life and you will call it fate.*
—Carl Jung

The temptation when reading any book on leadership is to skip to the diagrams, to the sections on "what to do," and directly apply a model or a technique to your leadership environment to "see if it works." This book, however, requires a different approach. It focuses on the essence of who we are and provides a sequential framework for exploring this in the context of contemplation. As we shine a light on our False Self and True Self, our growing awareness becomes the bedrock of any significant inner change that, in turn, affects our development as a leader. The practical work for you is to read with an open attitude, to bring your curiosity and a sense of possibility to what's contained in the pages that follow. You will likely encounter new tools and different perspectives on leadership than what you've seen before. But if these just remain "interesting ideas," then you will not develop as a contemplative leader; of most importance is that you might become aware of new dimensions within yourself. Completing the exercises and practices at the end of each chapter will be crucial for any inner changes to occur. And as these changes become part of who you are, you'll integrate this contemplative presence into your daily leadership experiences, deepening your connection to the people and organizations you lead.

What follows in the chapters ahead is a framework for developing as a contemplative leader. We begin by considering the nature of contemplation and what it means for us in a leadership context.

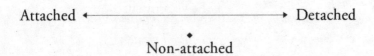

The first section of the book, "The Inner Journey of Contemplative Leadership," is a guide to examining the inner landscape of our lives as leaders. In chapter two, we consider the narratives that have shaped us and the cyclical nature of change that's part of our development. We complete an exercise that deconstructs the origins of our leadership narratives, creating the space to author new narratives as we move forward. Chapter three looks at the physiological underpinnings of our leadership presence. It outlines the different nervous-system states that influence our moment-by-moment awareness and how these affect our capacity to lead. Then, chapter four asks us to reflect on our experiences of challenge and failure in our leadership. Building on the insights of the previous chapters, we integrate growth-mindset research and examine the roles that fear, shame, and guilt can play in unconsciously shaping the choices we make as leaders.

In chapter five, we look at some of the underlying values and beliefs that shape our everyday behaviors. As part of this, we are introduced to the Logical Levels model of personal change, which can help us understand some of the dynamics and interconnections between our False Self and True Self.

This model[6] helps us frame the conscious as well as the unconscious aspects of who we are as leaders, who we've learned to become to "fit in," and who we really are and long to bring to the forefront in how we lead. Chapter six looks at the interplay of the various roles and identities that unconsciously shape how we view ourselves and therefore how we show up and are present to others. It's predominantly focused on a powerful, creative exercise that helps us

Logical Levels and True and False Self

Environment

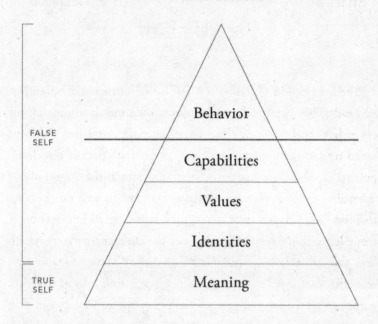

integrate all the work of the previous chapters. The final section of part one, chapter seven, ties all the content together by inviting us to reflect on our True Self. We examine the sense of meaning and purpose that we bring to each moment of our lives, the foundation of what inspires every leadership initiative in which we participate. This chapter introduces us to the Three Domes of Meaning, a simple yet profound model that frames all of the narratives of our leadership:[7] My Inner World (all of the work of part one of this book) in the context of My Outer World and Other Outer Worlds (all the people we lead and influence and interact with in our organizations and beyond) in the overall context of The Whole World (the bigger picture, all the interconnecting narratives and systems that exist, within which we live and lead).

The Three Domes of Meaning

The Whole World

The Story

WHAT IS

The great patterns that are always true
Saves us from the illusions of "we" and the smallness of "me"

My Outer World
& Other Outer Worlds

Our Story

WE ARE

Group identities and loyalties that expand our sense of self
Group ontology and epistemology, our narratives
Nationalism, cultural religion, and philosophy
Ethnicity, groupthink

My Inner World

My Story

I AM

The narrative of my life experiences
My "script" and how I face
challenge and "failure"
My autonomic nervous system states
My values and beliefs
My identities (my personas and their shadow)
My sense of meaning and purpose
**My False Self and True Self all together
(My Whole Self)**

Why I lead

The second part of the book, "The Outer Journey of Contemplative Leadership," provides some approaches to connect our inner contemplative leadership presence with the individuals, groups, and teams with whom we work. We begin chapter eight by looking at some of the fundamental dynamics of interpersonal relationships and reflect on how to connect our contemplative presence with others. Chapter nine then considers how we lead groups of people with a contemplative presence, the role of psychological safety in team development, and a multifaceted approach to identifying and improving trust. In chapter ten, we consider the leadership applications of Spiral Dynamics, a framework for the evolution of leadership that encompasses My Inner World, Our Outer World, and The Whole World. The book closes with a chapter that integrates the key exercises and learnings from each section. This prepares us to take our insights and practices and integrate our contemplative presence into the daily leadership situations we encounter.

Chapter 1

WHAT IS CONTEMPLATION?

*Contemplatives are individuals who live in and
return to the center within themselves, and yet they
know that they are not the Center. They are only a
part, but a gracious and grateful part at that.*
—Richard Rohr[1]

R ichard Rohr is an international speaker and author, long-time social activist, and founder of the Center for Action and Contemplation in New Mexico. He's a Franciscan friar, a dear friend, and the humblest leader I know. I've witnessed his humility firsthand on many occasions, but one instance stands out. We were meeting for coffee the morning after he hosted the biggest conference of his life, with five thousand in-person attendees flying in from all over the world to hear him speak for three days.

"You must be tired. What are you going to do for the rest of the week?" I asked.

"I'm driving down to El Paso to work with the migrants for ten days," he said. "After a weekend like that, I have to remember what's real."

Several years later, I reminded him about his retort, and he said, "It's dangerous to be worshiped; when you're on the stage, the person with the answer, the person who's admired—it does a number to your *ego*. And I need to go to a world like the border where no one knows me, no one knows I'm a priest or a teacher. And that puts my ego back in shape, a little bit at least . . . If I don't serve someone else, I take my importance far too seriously. It's all a myth, which I get attached to."

In the early 1980s, Richard shifted the focus of his work from community building and social activism to a form of leadership in action that embraces contemplation. He is widely regarded as one of the foremost teachers of contemplation in the world. "Contemplation is a different way of approaching the moment," says Richard. "Not in a demanding, manipulative way, but in a calm, receptive, and positive way. It's a way of enjoyment of the moment for what it is instead of forcing it to be what I feel I need. It's a way of seeing, it's a way of feeling, that has to be developed. It *can* be developed."

As a high-school student, Richard continued to encounter the word "contemplation" in the writings of the American monk Thomas Merton. "He used the word so much but doesn't really teach how to do it. He just keeps praising contemplation, and you experience it in his attitude towards reality." According to Richard, Merton's attitude wasn't

either/or thinking, it was both/and thinking. And that only came to me after years of reading him, how he thought more creatively, more positively, than most authors I read . . . Then, thirty-five years ago, I moved out here to New Mexico, and I began to study the teachings and the writings of the Trappist monk Thomas Keating. He described what I now call non-dual thinking, and he gave

*people practices to learn it, to think not either/or but to think both/
and. So, he brought the word "contemplation" to a very practical
level for me, and for a lot of other people, too.*

When asked about why he shifted his leadership focus from
being an activist to being a contemplative activist, Richard said that
it was because he had encountered "so many activists, doers, who
were so impatient and angry. Often very cynical—and I got tired of
that cynicism in myself and in others." He began to ask the questions "How can we still be active, serving, caring of all people, but
do it in a non-pushy way? How can we do it in a way that allows the
moment to unfold instead of forcing the moment?" Reflecting on
the practical ways he learned to answer these questions, Richard says
that a big part of his own learning was by being around people who
he felt were contemplative. "If I were honest," he says, "the best way
you learn it is to have some models in your life, of people who see
contemplatively. I learned it by meeting people who were that way,
who cared for the same causes, but did it with a half smile on their
face. Or could wait for [things] to unfold. They were much more
patient with others and with themselves."

Richard's work as a teacher, activist, and then a writer was well
known in certain circles for many years, but his fame and influence
have skyrocketed over the past decade. Leaders from a variety of
backgrounds—from rock stars to actors, billionaire philanthropists
to financiers—come to him for guidance. He has given talks at Google, been a guest on podcasts with Brené Brown, and been featured
on Oprah Winfrey's *Super Soul Sunday*. At some point in each talk or
interview, he invariably mentions the importance of contemplation
as a way of seeing and being.

The difference that contemplation has made in his leadership,
Richard explains, is that he does "not allow things to tie me up in
confusion or anger as easily. I still get resentful at the state of the

world . . . at the state of my own consciousness. But, to be honest, not for long. Now I learn to see the negative energy in myself, and I try to know the same moment, the same event, but in a different way. In a way that is compassionate, less judgmental. I'm happier. You're doing yourself a favor!" When he thinks back to himself as a much younger man, he says, "I was making it hard for some people to like me by my immense idealism and drivenness, my workaholism, and perfectionism. It might have made me feel heroic, but it was proba-bly terrible for others."

As he reflects on his leadership style, Richard says, "By nature, I'm a critical thinker. That serves me well as a teacher and analyst, but it doesn't serve me well in terms of being understanding, patient, lov-ing . . . You don't need to change reality to your liking—you *want* to, but you don't need to act on it right away. Everybody is attached to our way of thinking, and we're attached to wanting our conclusions to be operative right now."

As we discussed the nature of leadership, the requirement to complete tasks and deliver results, I asked Richard for his take on how leaders can lead in challenging times, how they can work with people who are not performing well and yet interact with them from this contemplative, nonjudgmental space:

I think it comes down to patience, that the way a leader addresses situations shows patience with growth, with development, with change, with how things unfold. And other people can feel that. You know the ideal, what other people want, and you find ways to say that, but it's much less demanding of the other person, it's much less insisting on "Now, now it has to happen" . . . Willful people will get you to do the right thing, but you feel shoved around, pushed around. Willing people are "allowers": they let it happen, they encourage it to happen, and then stand by and watch it. How can you lead, which in some degrees expects that you speak with authority and knowledge and clarity about direction, if you're not that, you're not a leader? We all think. Is there a way of doing that that isn't egocentric, isn't pushy? [It requires] a little inviting of the other person into agreement. It's always moving from insisting to inviting. Gazing instead of glaring or glancing.

Casting his mind back to his original leadership approach, Richard suspects that those he led thought that he was "in love with himself and his ideas more than with [them]." But over the years, as his thinking developed, as his presence changed, so did the quality of his interactions with others. "Contemplation," says Richard, "allows you to communicate love. I don't know if you *can* communicate love with anyone without doing it in a contemplative way. Otherwise, you do it in a utilitarian way, a pragmatic, problem-solving way. You can feel the pushiness, you can feel the judgmentalism in that—the other person can, or the group can."

Over time, as he "detached from [his] own ego," he developed "the ability to see [his] own flaws, to laugh at [himself], to be self-denigrating." Slowly, those he led began to see a significant change. He was moving from his driven, idealistic, perfectionistic leadership to something a lot more open and accepting. Others experienced less of his "pushiness" and "demanding" nature and more of "a soulful allowing." Richard says, "You know soulful people when you're around them; your energy changes, you feel accepted, you feel compassionately forgiven. This person will not judge me."

Thinking back over his eighty years of life, he summed up the difference contemplation has made for him: "I have a much higher ability to let go of my own agenda, of my own explanation. I have a much greater ability to see my own faults . . . It's now fairly easy for me to ask for forgiveness, to say I'm sorry when I know I did it wrong. I hope I'm more compassionate with myself, but I hope [also] with other people."

CONTEMPLATION AS NONATTACHMENT

Every country has its own cultural ideal of what success looks like and the way things should be: what we should aspire to, where we should grow in our work, and what kind of development is, therefore, required of us as leaders. For me, success was about hard work and the successful achievement of specific goals during each year of my life. For other leaders I know, it was about getting a profession and then having job security, societal prestige, and the ability to support up to three generations of their family. One way or another, we are all taught to aspire to some cultural narrative around "success." And over time, we become attached to this narrative.

When we become attached to *any* narrative, we start to identify with it to the exclusion of other narratives. We derive a sense of identity, value, and self-worth from living out that story. Some narratives have specific roles attached to them: "I'm a doctor, a director, a senior vice president, a congresswoman." We see ourselves as a particular kind of person, a certain type of leader. We compare ourselves to an ideal and strive to become the epitome of whatever role or title we deem necessary to live successfully.

But the more we attach to this ideal, the more we *need* it to be true of us, and the more—as Richard alluded to—we force ourselves, push others, and seek control of our environments to make sure we achieve our goals by earning a promotion or a bonus, securing funding for our cause, gaining market share for our corporation, winning an election, or hitting whatever our latest goal is. Yet, as we become more attached to achieving success, we can easily become disconnected from ourselves, from what we want, and from who we really are.

The following diagram illustrates this simple but important concept. One end of the continuum represents being totally attached, where we need to be in control and get what we want. We'll do whatever it takes to make this happen. The other end of the continuum is where we're totally detached, where we've stopped caring altogether and disengage from pursuing something that was once important to us:

Attached ←——————————————→ Detached

It has to happen   I don't care if it happens

When we're used to success and have had years of experiences where we felt in control, we build up the muscle memory doing things our way. Seemingly mature and wise leaders can become petulant in an instant if they're outvoted by their board. Hardworking activists and executives alike can completely detach from the goals they've worked toward for many years. When we want something so badly that we believe we *need* to have it, we set ourselves up to have our self-worth determined by the degree of success we achieve. As Richard says, we get used to being "the person with the answer, the person who's admired."

The more attached we are to a particular outcome, the more prone we are to experiencing constant low-level anxiety. Over time, this develops into the type of stress ("distress") that inhibits our performance and eventually puts us firmly on the path toward burnout.[2] The more stress we carry into each moment, the more fearful we can become to make decisions. We start to overthink things in areas where, in the past, we would have simply decided and moved on. This pressure to perform can give rise to behaviors different from our norm; we might become pushy or impatient with others, manipulative, or even deceitful. This can lead to relational breakdowns with those we are close to in our teams or wider organizations and with clients, mentors, and others who care about us. We become more controlling of tiny details in our daily lives; for example, we might relentlessly control our schedule or our workspace and micromanage the work of others. We lose our temper if we don't get our way. We unintentionally bully others. Our conversations become more about being *right* than doing what's best for our organization. We stray off topic when someone disagrees with us, shifting our focus from the issues at hand to making the conversation a critique of the other person. Being attached to a narrative of success, insisting on having *our* way and achieving *our* goals, can eventually result in our feeling stuck. We lose touch with what's most important to us and to the people around us.

From working with many leaders across various industries, I have noticed that when this level of attachment is maintained for long periods of time, leaders often spend more time on the "hamster wheel of activity" at work, putting in extra hours while getting less and less done, stressing more and more, and not spending any personal time in recreation. The very idea of *re-creation*, taking time for themselves to reconnect with a renewed energy for life, is beyond their capacity to imagine or enact. When asked about why they continue through this struggle, many comment on feeling trapped: "I can't leave," "I can't afford to stop," "My family relies on me," or "There's nothing else I'm trained to do." They are in Samuel Beckett's bind, feeling that "You must go on, I can't go on, I'll go on."[3]

The typical cycle around this is to pendulum swing from being very attached to being very detached. We overidentify with a role, a task, a project, and then when we don't get what we had hoped for, we swing all the way in the opposite direction until we no longer identify with what we once really wanted. It's a very natural defense mechanism that protects us from feeling disappointed when we don't achieve our goals or feeling hurt when relationships break down. But this "yo-yoing" from attachment to detachment is an unstable place from which to lead. It not only impacts us personally as we become stressed and pressurized, then deflated and depressed; it also deeply affects the people we lead. Those who rely on us, who look to us for guidance, can never know what version of us they'll encounter. They learn to walk on eggshells, to be guarded in their interactions with us, until they know how best to proceed.

THE ALTERNATIVE

We need to step off this attached–detached continuum and onto a different plane entirely. We need to learn to become nonattached.

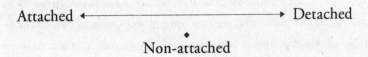

In this book, I use the word "contemplation" as a synonym for nonattachment. When we are nonattached, we are present to whatever is here, within me, with others, in this whole situation. We are open to new perspectives. Rather than projecting our lenses and our wishes onto this moment, we bring a curious, accepting presence to what is *here*. We recognize the struggles of the colleague we're speaking with rather than immediately trying to create a plan for them to change. We pay attention to the developmental feedback our team has for us rather than blaming a difficult trading environment for our performance as a leader.

When applied to a leadership context, nonattachment means that we do not need our perspective to be right or to be the only perspective. It allows us to be open to other perspectives and processes than those we might have used in the past. This kind of approach and attitude allows us to test and experiment with team dynamics and with the people and systems with which we work. For example, we might start asking open-ended questions and paying attention to the different answers and perspectives we receive. Instead of having to find the right answer straight away, we might notice where we're leaning right now and remain open to seeing how that will land with other stakeholders. We might become more open to letting situations evolve, to allowing solutions to emerge.

The fundamental belief and trust of contemplation is that, through this attitude and practical approach of nonattachment, we can "get out of the way" and allow the present moment to unfold in better ways than we could have planned. It involves a trust that something good can happen and that we can participate in it by resisting the temptation to exert our control. Our perspectives are so limited (to the point that we can only process about 60–120 megabits of data out of an available field of 1.2 gigabytes that are available to our five senses every second[4]) that our attempts to take control are always going to be myopic. But when we lead through contemplation, from a place of nonattachment, we engage with more relevant data and more easily focus on the available opportunities and possibilities in our leadership environment. And an important element in cultivating this capacity to see clearly, to be present, is engaging in contemplative practices.

PRACTICES

To develop a contemplative way of being requires us to find ways to self-regulate our emotions and connect to our inner and outer worlds. Whether it's spending time alone in nature, reading, exercising, playing music, enjoying a glass of wine with friends, or meditating, we need to uncover and develop the lifestyle practices that help us reconnect, time and again, with our Whole Self. Broadly speaking, contemplative practices come in two categories: formal and informal practices.

Formal practices are the regular activities, such as a contemplative sit (also known as meditation), that build the muscle memory, habits, and brain changes that allow us to see from a contemplative viewpoint. Informal practices flow from these formal practices and include the way we listen to colleagues in meetings, how we speak to customers, and the open-minded responses we give when reading new information that we would have previously rejected out of hand. Investing time to cultivate both formal and informal practices is the bedrock of leading from a contemplative perspective. It's the equivalent of putting in the miles, as a runner does in anticipation of a long-distance race, or writing ten drafts before submitting a college essay assignment. The regular training and practice change us, developing our ability to respond to new demands in a resourceful way rather than reacting from a place of stress or a need to control.

What we know from recent research is that this practice of contemplative sits (one form of which is Mindfulness training) helps to physically change the structure of our brain.[5] When practiced for a continuous period (eight weeks in a row[6]), there is a densification of neurons in the frontal lobe, which can lead to more effective and rational thinking.[7] There are also decreased levels of emotional reactivity because of changes in the size of the amygdala and the hippocampus in the brain's limbic system.[8] This leaves us less likely to react in an unhelpful way under pressure, and when we do react in stressful situations, our sense of vigilance won't last for as long as it would have before we were engaging in contemplative practices.[9]

Richard says of a contemplative sit, "A 'sit' is a word we learn from Buddhism; it doesn't have the penitential connotations of 'kneel'; it has the connotations of 'sit and wait calmly.' It's a practice, just like the piano or basketball; you have to practice for hours, for years, to become good. Athletes know that; musicians know that . . . At the end of the twenty minutes [of sit], I'm usually energetically different. I can half-smile at everything, at myself, at the seeming mistakes of other people. You change your energy from anal-retentive pushiness, demanding, to a soulful allowing."

GUIDED CONTEMPLATIVE SIT/MEDITATION

Some have called a contemplative sit an exercise in futility, as it's "unproductive" time, usually filled with the many interruptions of our thoughts. When I engage in the silence of a contemplative sit, I often have myriad thoughts throughout, noticing what I'm worried about or thinking about my schedule later that day. This is just my ego—another word for my False Self—trying to direct my attention and control my environment. And once I realize this, I'm able to let go of those thoughts and worries and return my focus back to being in the moment. It took me many weeks of practice before I was able to move beyond my constant, cyclical thoughts and instead focus on being present for more than a few seconds. But with contin-ued practice, I experienced more clarity and poise during my sits. I slowly developed the ability to acknowledge my thoughts, worries, and concerns, to thank them for coming into my consciousness, and to tell them that I'd return to them later but that, for now, I was focusing my attention on this contemplative sit. Sometimes I'd focus on my breath; other times I'd focus on a sensation or a particular place in my body to help me return my awareness to my sit. If practicing a sit for the first time, a helpful start is to focus on your inhale and exhale, as well as all the other sensations you feel in your body as you breathe. Some people like to silently repeat a gen-tle mantra to themselves, a short, meaningful phrase that reminds them of the importance of their presence as foundational to anything they do (e.g., "Everything I need is here"). The choice is yours.

After a few years of practice, a friend of mine taught me at the end of each sit to stand up, look down at my seat, and acknowledge the various thoughts, fears, and concerns I've had. I then thank my ego/my False Self, for making me aware of these areas of my life where I want to be in control, and, bowing to my ego/False Self in gratitude, I tell them that I'm going to leave them here, on this seat, while I move into the next part of my day.

1. Read over the following script for a self-guided contemplative sit (or ask someone to read it to you). You will need a countdown timer (a clock or a cell phone timer). Having a meditation bell (a digital or physical bell) to indicate the start and end of the contemplative sit is recommended but not necessary. You can sound the meditation bell and start the countdown timer once you finish reading the script below, pausing after each phrase. Some people find it helpful to close their eyes during the silence of the sit. The instructions in parentheses are guidelines for you and do not have to be read aloud.[10]

   If this is your first time engaging in a contemplative sit, I suggest starting with two to five minutes of silence after reading the script aloud. Over time, with daily practice, this can increase to as many as twenty minutes per day.

   ### Script for Self-Guided Contemplative Sit:
   As I begin my contemplative sit, I take a few moments to notice my posture. Becoming comfortable in my seat, I sit slightly forward so that my spine is no longer touching the back of the seat. I become aware of my feet touching the floor, grounding me in the present moment. I focus on my back and

*neck, allowing them to find their most aligned and neutral
positions.*

*I remember that I'm not trying to achieve anything. There
are no goals. I am simply becoming aware of my presence in
this moment. Noticing any distractions, thoughts, judgments,
decisions, and ideas that cross my mind, and paying attention
to any emotions that I feel. I choose to let go of all these for
now. Instead, I focus on my moment-by-moment experience
of being present to what is, to both the expansiveness of the
universe and to the sensations of my body in this seat, in this
place, just here, right now.*

*When I become distracted, frustrated, or confused, I con-
sciously return to simply focusing on my breath—in and out.
I know that deep presence is already within me, whether I'm
aware of it or not. No reaching or striving is required—my
only work is to be as present as I can be to myself, to this place,
and to this moment right now.*

(Now read the following text aloud, pausing after each
line. The silent portion of your sit will follow.)

Be still and allow this moment to envelop you
Be still and allow this moment
Be still and allow
Be still
Be

(Now start the countdown timer and ring a meditation
bell to indicate that the contemplative sit has begun. Ring
the bell again to indicate that the contemplative sit has
finished after two, five, ten, fifteen, or twenty minutes—
whichever time frame you have selected.)

2. Journal about what this experience was like.
3. Repeat this contemplative sit each day, ideally for a minimum of forty days, as practicing anything over this period helps us form a new habit.

Part I

THE INNER JOURNEY OF CONTEMPLATIVE LEADERSHIP

Chapter 2

OUR LEADERSHIP JOURNEY

It is by going down into the abyss that we recover the treasures of life. Where you stumble, there lies your treasure. The very cave you are afraid to enter turns out to be the source of what you are looking for. The damned thing in the cave that was so dreaded has become the center.

—Joseph Campbell[1]

The stories we tell ourselves, the narratives that describe the context of our lives, fundamentally affect the choices we make each day. For many of us, the narrative of the "hero" leader has been a foundational story that has impacted our life choices. We have been raised in a society that values competition, personally overcoming great obstacles, and finding ways to pick ourselves up when we fail so that we can ultimately overcome. This narrative ends up finding its way into many aspects of our lives, from sports to academic pursuits to how we engage in friendships and romantic relationships to the style and tone of how we lead and influence others.

For most who lead in the business or political world, this notion of the hero leader who overcomes and wins has been the dominant narrative that has fueled our rise through the ranks. One way of summarizing this storyline is that we believe we are part of a world in which only a zero-sum game exists, where there is always a clear winner and a clear loser. This narrative often comes from a place of fear where there is a perceived lack of available resources to go around. Losing represents insecurity and suffering, so winning is the logical necessity.

Louise Chester is a former London City banker who, when appointed, was the youngest director at UBS Ltd. By her early thirties, she had become the head of research and global head of media and telecoms at Dresdner RCM. To an outside observer, her career was stellar, easeful, seamless. But below the surface, her ability to lead in such a high-stress environment was underpinned by a set of practices and beliefs that were hard earned.

From childhood, Louise had had a strong sense that "life is sacred and it's an incredible privilege to be here." She felt she could choose "a life of meaning" and that with "every experience came the opportunity for a greater understanding to enable [her] to be more of service to others." But at the age of twenty, she was diagnosed with non-Hodgkin lymphoma and given potentially three months to live. "I had a strong sense that I hadn't really fulfilled what was important in my life, that I hadn't really taken my mission seriously," she explained to me. Then, the night before she was to start chemotherapy, her medical team called to say that they hadn't seen any cancer in her latest biopsy. "I felt the sadness of the life I'd missed, and it really made me think, 'I've been given another chance, and I'm not going to waste another day.'" Inspired by her grandmother and spurred on by her experience of cancer, Louise became a Buddhist.

Although she had founded and sold a small business during college, nothing else about her education or background had earmarked her for a senior role in financial services; she had middle-school math, high-school economics, and a degree in English literature. But she was determined to find her way in the City of London and, after a time spent answering calls and opening mail, she landed a job at a Japanese asset-management company managing a fund and doing exchange-rate and interest forecasts.

"I was this incredibly successful investment analyst in the City, and at the same time I was a practicing Buddhist, and it was my mission to show people that, if you take responsibility for your life, if you see your life as sacred and you try to really inspire people to be a beacon of hope for others, then you can live a life of meaning and of service," Louise said.

It soon became apparent that Louise's approach to work was quite different from that of other analysts. People started to ask her how she had developed her ability to zoom right in on the details of complex spreadsheets and then zoom out and see the bigger picture of global market trends. Her grandmother had taught her to meditate as a child, and it was during these early meditation experiences that Louise started to experience the capacity to "flex between deep, sharp focus and open awareness—to be able to hold both the micro to the macro at the same time in this kind of tension."

To discover what exactly was working so well for her, Louise looked at some of the early research into the neuroscience of meditation. "There was a piece of research done in Boston showing that meditation started to change the structure and function of your brain," she said. Looking at the conclusions, Louise grasped that practicing meditation made people less emotionally reactive to high-stress situations, increased their ability to focus on one task at a time, and more easily activated a part of the nervous system that brought with it a sense of curiosity and creativity, all of which resonated with Louise.

Based on her experience of meditation and this preliminary study on the effects it had on brain functioning, she designed a program so others could benefit from what was working so well for her. Louise knew she needed to develop something that was in no way religious but simply focused on demystifying the process of meditating:

> I wanted to embed in hundreds of thousands of people the ability to . . . be more conscious about the decisions they make and to take that responsibility. For the whole financial industry to come to an acknowledgement that good business is good business. And that if you want to invest for your pension, you want to invest for the long term and you want to invest in an organization that is overall purposeful. There's no point getting a high return from a transport company that you've invested in [if] the fumes from their lorries are giving your child asthma. I wanted to give people the ability to be more conscious, [to] not just focus on the outer game and on the doing but also to be able to zoom out and see and experience the bigger picture, the context in which we operate. So that's why I set up Mindfulness at Work, to take this very simple thing—a trojan horse—into organizations so that you open the hearts of people, and they then want to do good. The Buddha used expedient means, and as a bodhisattva, I knew I had to offer it in a way [that] was pragmatic.

Her first program was with the CEO of JPMorgan Private Bank in Knightsbridge. The head of learning from Ashurst, a law firm, came to observe and decided to take it on. That year, Mindfulness at Work won the Legal and Education Training Group award, sponsored by Ashurst, for Best Personal Development Program. And the company grew from there, working with almost 250 companies across all different sectors ever since. Louise is well placed to work with leaders, as she is personally aware of the challenges of being distracted and emotionally reactive while leading a company.

"When I get extremely upset about things, when something 'hijacks me,' and I become aware of it, it's very interesting for me. This is a gift of curiosity," Louise said. These regular experiences give Louise "that little bit of space to be able to experience things . . . to be a little bit dispassionate. It's sort of bringing that kind of beginner's mind to this moment and seeing what the moment will teach you, but without holding it as some kind of outcome, because I'm not necessarily looking for a solution. I'm looking to learn from the situation itself. And to have the patience to see that I might never know—and that's okay—I might never know why something is how it is. But it is a sort of surrendering to grace. If I try and control things, then I've closed off a possibility.

"The work I'm doing with other leaders is really around sitting in that muddy middle and choosing not to close down possibility by making things one thing or the other," Louise continued. "It's very easy to say other people are bad or they're wrong. And there's a sort of wanting to make things one way or the other, to create simplicity, but when you do, you close down possibility."

Reflecting on the essence of contemplative leadership, the reason why it's so crucially important for leaders to integrate it into their leadership practice, Louise asked:

> *How do we hone the skill of sitting down with people who we abhor and see their humanity? How do we notice our anger, our revulsion, our dismissal of them? Do we still sit there and see them as this human being who has a point of view, bring our curiosity, and truly listen . . . rather than just make assumptions? We need to learn to sit down together for the sake of humanity because, if not, we're just going to the polarities. The invitation for us is to really hold that incredibly difficult middle ground. And we can't hold it easily with our head because our head wants the binary. It wants*

the certainty at once. The one way or the other—it's almost like we have to hold it with our heart and our body.

For the last number of decades, leadership consultants and coaches have presented alternative narratives for leaders to embrace. There is a movement away from zero-sum games to win-win scenarios where relationships can be developed and outcomes emerge over time. One such alternate narrative is "situational leadership," which involves adapting our style to best fit the people we are working with and the context we are working within. This is just one way in which a leader does not have to be winning, all-knowing, or at the front to lead the charge. Instead, these narratives give permission for leaders to serve others, to share some responsibilities, and to adapt to scenarios based on the needs of those in front of them.

The hallmark of leading from a place of contemplation is that we are open to change, again and again, each time we look inside ourselves. One of the most challenging ways we change is by firstly becoming aware of the elements in our narrative that we need to let go of and then, in time, developing the courage to step into new narratives that more accurately match our leadership presence at this point in our lives. For this, we first need to become conscious of the stories we tell ourselves and the values that these stories engender in us. An overarching framework that helps with this process is Joseph Campbell's "monomyth" of the hero, or, as it's more commonly known today, the "Hero's Journey." Despite the name, it tells a very different hero story than that of a zero-sum game.

THE MONOMYTH OF THE HERO

Joseph Campbell was a scholar and educator who dedicated himself to the study and teaching of comparative mythology. He published many books throughout his life, but his 1949 classic, *The Hero with A Thousand Faces*, is his most famous. In it, Campbell outlines the fundamental importance of story, of the narratives that we each buy into. He compares and contrasts the stories, or mythologies, of various societies and cultures—from prehistory to modern times, stories ranging from Japan to India, Russia to Ireland, North America to the Pacific Islands. His central argument is all of these stories are variations on the same Hero's Journey.

Broadly summarized, there are three distinctive yet interconnected phases to the Hero's Journey: Departure, Descent, and Return. Reflecting on our experiences of these three phases of the Hero's Journey is really helpful for us to understand the narratives that we live by and how these narratives affect the ways in which we lead. As we learn to lead from a place of contemplation, of nonattachment, to control certain outcomes in our realm of influence, the Hero's Journey framework helps us to see our reality more clearly. It empowers us to reinterpret the narrative of our leadership, most especially if we feel like our world is falling apart. This helps us realize that it is *not* falling apart; it's simply being reordered. And our willingness to participate in this reordering—or our fight against it—will qualitatively affect our daily experiences of how we lead ourselves and how we show up for others.

Situating ourselves within an overarching narrative, locating which phase of the Hero's Journey most resonates for us now, can be a very powerful way of understanding the overall context of our leadership development.

As I outline the various elements within these three phases, I encourage you to think about a challenge that you are currently facing, or have recently faced, in your own leadership. Break this challenge down to as many of the steps of the Hero's Journey as possible, and notice what insights this exercise may bring.

1. DEPARTURE FROM OUR NORMAL WORLD

Before we make any changes to our leadership, it's important to first take stock and become aware of our version of "normal." What have we been socialized to expect to be a normal set of scenarios in which we lead? This goes far beyond the culture of our organization and our expectations for growth, promotion, or salary. This has more to do with the overarching narrative of our society and the factors that led us to leading and influencing in the first place.

What each of us expects to see happen in our career, in our life's work, can be very different. This is affected by two key concepts: ontology and epistemology,

Ontology is the study of the nature of being. Deriving from the Greek word *ont*, "being," and the Medieval Latin suffix *ology*, the study of a body of knowledge, this "study of being" asks some profound questions of us: Why are we here? Why are we alive? Different cultures and societies provide differing views on these questions. For some, it's to live a life of pleasure and ease. For others, it's to honor those who have gone before us with the life choices we make today. Still others point to living in harmony with our environment and making choices that will benefit seven generations into the future.

In the Western world, leaders often use the language of "finding meaning" and "discovering purpose" when describing their own interpretation of ontology, why they believe their leadership is important. But for us to understand why we believe we are here and what is our work to do, we must also examine our epistemology, the sources we trust to tell us that our ontology is true.

Epistemology is the study of knowledge. *Episteme* comes from the Greek, meaning "knowledge" or "understanding." What bodies of knowledge, what sacred texts, legal texts, and other books and stories do we hold to be true? What institutions and authority figures, such as business leaders, teachers, family members, politicians, pop idols, authors, and other role models, do we trust to tell us that our version of reality is justified? *Can* we trust these sources, or have we ever questioned them at all? When things are going our way, we usually don't consider questioning the sources of knowledge that back up the narratives we have for why we lead. But when things get challenging, when we face a global downturn or a pandemic, or when the implications of climate change directly affect our product or the viability of the services we provide, then we might start to question the underlying assumptions that we have.

I attended a school where the standard narrative from parents and teachers was that if we worked hard in school and across our career, ideally in a profession, then some of us would become very wealthy as a result. In my context, where society didn't have a clearly defined class system, being wealthy equated with being powerful. This was the first ontology that I adopted for myself, my first *raison d'être*, and one I pursued for several years. The affirming attitudes of the teachers in my school, the success-oriented behaviors of the parents of my classmates, and the wider societal support of this way of life provided the epistemological sources I needed to assure me that my focus was correct.

But, coming from a different kind of background, I was an outlier in this context, not coming from a family that recognized professions or wealth. So as a thirteen-year-old, with my classmates living in big homes, having multiple annual vacations, and talking about their parents' businesses, this version of "normal" was all new to me. My values were shaped during my time at school as I was exposed to this dominant culture that emphasized hard work and wealth as prerequisites to career success. Therefore, leadership was, originally to my understanding, a way of thinking and acting that could advance one's career and life to the point of bringing wealth and success. That was my starting point, and it took a lot of trial and error, failure, and loss for me to eventually question this original narrative that I had assumed was absolutely good and right.

In college, I met people with very different narratives. One friend had no interest in building his career or accumulating wealth and power. Instead, he wanted to develop his talents and apply his gifts so that he could best contribute to society as a social worker. Others I have encountered in my coaching work have had different narratives as well; one woman discussed how she had come from a wealthy family in India, where her father was a diplomat and, because of conversations with him and his colleagues, she had devoted herself to leading in the humanitarian sector. But she then transferred to the corporate sector so that she could reinvest the assets of her employer's company to deliver clean water to millions of people in developing countries. Her new leadership narrative straddled the for-profit and the not-for-profit sectors. Ask yourself these questions to uncover some elements of the narratives that influenced your expectations of leadership:

- What narratives most shaped your own leadership during your early life?
- What has always seemed like a normal narrative of how your life should go?

The Departure from our Normal World stage of the Hero's Journey takes place when something happens that leads us to question the narratives that we once held to be undeniably true. We lose our job, we don't get a promotion, our project goes wrong, we are criticized by a mentor. Or perhaps we achieve our goals or fulfill the objectives of the narratives we have for ourselves but are left feeling a little empty inside. We make our first million, we IPO, we sell our stake in the firm, we lead a team to achieve stellar success, we land a major client. *Now what? Surely there's more than this.*

Developmental psychologists from Erik Erikson to Clare Graves talk about the need to transcend one phase of life to enter into another. We need a new narrative to continue forward. But some-times we don't know what new paradigm, what new story, to step into. The way ahead can feel unclear; there may be no clean and crisp approach that seems to fit. We only know that we must step away and go somewhere else. This is the invitation to the Descent.

2. DESCENT

According to the Hero's Journey, to cross the threshold and enter into the unknown, many—if not all of us—need a little bit of support, or a little bit of a push from someone who has already gone ahead of us and experienced their own Hero's Journey. This person is known as a mentor and takes their name from Homer's *Odyssey*. According to this ancient story, before departing to fight in the Trojan War, King Odysseus instructed his trusted advisor, named Mentor, to raise his son, Telemachus. Mentor's task is to lead and guide, encourage, and admonish the young boy so he can mature into a man. In our own leadership-development story, our mentor is someone we respect, who has experienced far more than us, and who takes a personal interest in supporting us to learn and develop along the path ahead. They may provide advice, practical training, personal support, or an opportunity that allows us to take our first tentative steps in a new direction. Fundamental to any good mentor is that they know the territory ahead and are personally invested in seeing us learn to nav-igate it by ourselves.

In my experience of coaching and running mentoring programs within organizations, very few leaders get to experience helpful and healthy mentoring. Official mentors are often toeing the party line, preventing us from moving away from the narratives that no longer serve us. It takes a rare, courageous, and open person to truly men-tor other leaders. In the absence of being mentored, reading books, watching videos, and listening to podcasts of other leaders we respect can be a good alternative.

When Louise was twenty, her cancer diagnosis precipitated her Departure from her Normal World into a Descent. She not only suffered physically; the emotional and psychological pain also led her to conclude that she "hadn't really taken [her] mission" seriously. Memories of times spent with her grandmother inspired her, and, combined with encounters with her Buddhist neighbors, this led to the complete reevaluation of her narrative. It's painful to Depart from our Normal World. We leave safety and security behind. We enter unknown territory, which, by its very nature, can be a fearful experience. But this is necessary, as—in the case of Louise and many others—this facing of fears is metamorphic, sowing the seeds of a new narrative and a new way of leading and contributing.

One of the key themes of the Hero's Journey is that, in moving from Departure into Descent, we come face-to-face with our fears: loss of status, loss of monetary certainty, exposure of our flaws, or whatever they may be. Acknowledging our fears can be an unsettling experience. It requires vulnerability and courage. Vulnerability comes from the Latin *vulnus*, a wound. We are vulnerable when we acknowledge that there are chinks in our armor and that we carry wounds. In this context, admitting that we have fears is an act of vulnerability. Acknowledging this is a critical first step, as only then can we do something about those fears.

Courage comes from the Latin *cor*, "heart," and *agere*, "to act." I think of courage as choosing "to act with heart," to do something in a way that brings the core of our being, our True Self, to the fore.

We need a lot of courage to both face our fears head-on and then act with heart and do something constructive with them. Campbell says that

> *The very cave you are afraid to enter turns out to be the source of what you are looking for.*[2]

Having the courage to face our fears bring our True Self to the fore.

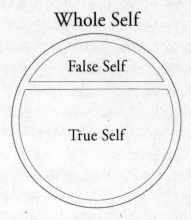

Whole Self

When a mentor offers to guide and support us, it's important that they are not peddling some quick-fix solution. One of the hallmarks of a great mentor is that they help us focus on *why* we're stumbling with our old narratives and support us as we go "down into the abyss [to] recover the treasures of life."[3] It can be frightening to call our leadership narratives into question. It's difficult for our ego, too, as we will feel out of control—and we *will* be out of control. But once we have committed ourselves to this path of Descent, once we open ourselves up to seeing what emerges into our consciousness, we create the conditions that allow new narratives and new perspectives on leadership to develop.

It's not an easy path. Maintaining the status quo of our Normal World might be much easier, if less rewarding. This phase of Descent involves us coming face-to-face with our need for control and acknowledging that wanting to feel in control helps us deal with our fears. This is a great starting point for surviving daily life, but we're now being invited away from a reactive approach to leadership to something more considered, more responsive, more of an overflow of our inner presence into connection with our external world.

Two Kinds of Suffering

On a recent episode of *The High Performance Podcast*, former English rugby captain and World Cup winner Jonny Wilkinson talked about the "fragility of people that believe in themselves. Look at anyone that's in the middle of self-belief; you'll see someone who's covering up fear."[4] As a world-renowned athlete, considered the very best of his generation, Wilkinson and his career revolved around a narrative whereby he always had to win, constantly grow, and believe that "leaving a legacy after [he was] gone is what [would] bring joy."

"I mean, it's ludicrous," said Wilkinson. "And that's kind of where I was. You know, my whole rugby career was like, 'I'm going to suffer through this because I'm going to leave the greatest mark.'"

Broadly speaking, there are two types of suffering we can experience. The first is when we choose to make sacrifices and to suffer so that something better can happen as a result of our leadership. Our choosing to suffer produces a benefit for us and for others. Wilkinson put it very eloquently when he talked about how he had worked incredibly hard on and off the pitch and that his narrative, in his own words, had been one that said, "When I grow up, when I get my car, when I get my promotion, when I get my big house, when I get to retirement—that's when my joy is going to hit me, when I've got enough money."[5] But even when he had achieved so much success in his career and personal life, he was "still suffering and stressing for the next thing."[6] It took him some time to realize that he had been deeply unhappy living within his old narrative of winning and compulsively improving to the next level of leadership and personal performance. "It's like, well, what happens to just flourishing, enjoying and loving life?"

The second type of suffering is when things "go wrong," when external factors outside of our control move us away from our current trajectory and lead us down a path we have never intended to tread. We develop a health issue, a family member dies unexpectedly, our relationship breaks down irreconcilably, we lose our job, an important project falls apart, our company folds. The fleeting nature of life resounds all around and within us, and we have no choice but to sit with some stark realities of loss, to sit with an unexpected source of deep pain. Our world is thrown into disarray. We question the narratives we've held on to for so long. We wonder about the trustworthiness of the books, the role models, the institutions that seemed to be so sure of themselves, that had assured us of a secure and compelling source of truth.

Most of us face this second category of suffering several times in our lives. For some, it happens early; for others, it happens often. But not everyone learns from this kind of suffering. I have witnessed many leaders who did not learn from their experiences of suffering—they blocked it out, they refused to face it, they redoubled their efforts at work and made success at their role their most important narrative. They overworked to numb the pain of suffering in other areas of their lives. And, as a result, they got "stuck"; they became immovable in their convictions and approaches.

I recently worked with a business leader who kept on returning to the topic of his marriage falling apart. And whenever we explored this topic, he explained that it was a result of him not leading the business well enough and not earning enough money. Over several months, we returned to this same narrative again and again. When we'd talk about leading his business, he'd say he couldn't focus because his marriage was on the rocks; when we'd talk about his marriage, he'd say it was because he wasn't earning enough money since he wasn't leading the business well enough. He was really suffering, both professionally and personally. The story he told himself, the narrative he had, framed himself as not being a "good enough" earner, causing himself ongoing pain. It began to emerge that he wasn't listening well to his co-owner or to his people in the business and that he wasn't listening to his wife very well, either.

Richard Rohr talks about the futility of trying to control the suffering we experience during Descent as being like trying to control the flow of the Big River in which we're swimming.[7] What we need, instead, is to tune in to the flow of the water and allow ourselves to go with it.

Floating down this river, we can easily focus on how much we are not in control and struggle to get back to where we first entered the water. We try swimming upstream, going against the flow, which frustrates and exhausts us. But then we reach a point where we finally accept the river's flow and shift our focus to the experience of floating downstream. Yes, we are leaving behind familiar vistas of places that we know like the back of our hand. But we're having a new, embodied experience of going with the Big River, of being caught up in something much more than just ourselves, which brings us to new places and new vistas at every turn. We're part of the flow. But whether we fight it—always swimming to the side to get onto the riverbank—or go with it will fundamentally affect what happens within us and where we end up.

It's the same for the processes of leadership coaching. What happens during the process and where we get to at the end are fundamentally affected by how we participate at each step. I've worked with people during a phase of Descent who fight me and fight the process, and our progress is very slow. They question the parameters of the process, question themselves, and undermine the work that they *say* they want to do. They look for ways to get back to what they know, to how they once lived. But by continually wanting something else, they're not fully present to what is here right now. As a result of trying to control the process, they miss out on what is emerging in this moment.

This Descent away from the normality of how we've lived and led before is disorienting and usually fills us with a sense of loss and pain. We've spent so much time and energy defining ourselves by how well we're living the first narrative we learned that we feel like we'll lose a part of our very selves if we let it go. Professional athletes often struggle to know who they are after they retire from sports. Organizational leaders often have a hard time when they step away from their high-intensity corporate environment to start an equally high-intensity parental leave. Political leaders have been known to crumble when they lose their seats.

Our ego is made up of all the different identities, known as "personas," that we have taken on as part of living out our primary narrative. Examples of a persona include a high-performing athlete, a driven corporate leader, and a service-oriented politician. There's nothing *wrong* with any of these personas; they can be very helpful. When we're growing up and maturing, these various personas give us something to aim for; they motivate us; they help us feel like we've arrived somewhere. There's nothing like seeing the pride of a first-year medical student, a newly appointed corporate leader, or a politician winning their seat for the first time—it's exhilarating. But if we grow too attached to these identities, these personas, then we cannot let go of them and be slightly less defined by them as we grow older and more mature. The stronger our attachment to these identities, the more difficult it will be for us to embrace this stage of the Descent, and the more we'll fight to cling to them, insisting on remaining in control rather than going with the flow of the Big River.

3. RETURN

Wilkinson talked about his experience of transition from the Descent into the Return stage of the Hero's Journey. He said that he has been on a fifteen-year journey, "with nowhere else to turn but inwards," exploring the fears that once shaped his daily life. He is now "willing to be open to the future and say . . . Let's just see . . . Why not just live now all of the time?"[8]

In his own words, this exploration of the cave of fears that under-pinned his original Normal World narrative has brought him to a place where there are "no boundaries. All I've found is opportunity, space, and deeper dimensions of experience."

This is what happens when we embrace the phase of Descent and discover what it might teach us. Eventually, at a time and in a way that we cannot fully understand or plan, something emerges from within. We have sat with our pain, we have faced loss, and we have faced disappointment. We've experienced a kind of "death"—the loss of a career; a health issue; an injury; the definitive end of a relationship; the loss of our job, our status, our company, our role of perceived significance in life. It could even be the loss of face from an error of judgment that affected our reputation as a leader. But somewhere from within this death, something else emerges—slowly, and usually in surprising ways.

We have learned that there's more to us and more to life than what we had previously realized. The old narrative of why we were living and the old sources of authority that told us, "This is the best way to live," have been transcended. We don't necessarily have to get rid of our old narratives entirely. But as we have developed, there is now a broader and deeper container within which our old narratives fit. We are more than our achievements, and we are more than our roles. We realize that we are only one small part of the Big River, and this fills us with a sense of freedom and ease.[9]

We cannot force this change to occur. It is "done unto us." The Descent strips away everything that is unnecessary, reminding us of what's most important about who we are and how we lead. Then, contemplative practices—from meditation to walks in nature to journaling, or anything that re-grounds us into who we are in this moment—help to keep us in shape. These practices are the equivalent of strength and conditioning workouts to athletes; they are the foundation upon which all other training and performance is based.

Finally, moving from the Descent into the Return is something that happens *to* us when we are ready. It slowly emerges from within, with a surprisingly calm energy that invites us to be more present to ourselves in this moment and more connected with others and with our environment. We move away from narrow narratives about how life *should* be to more expansive narratives that give us and others a spaciousness to live with a greater sense of freedom and possibility. As we Return, we notice our emotional state, how we feel interacting with others, how we feel within ourselves. We pay attention to our thoughts, including automatic negative thoughts or default thinking patterns that limit us and those we lead and influence.

When we remove preconceived narratives and ideas of how things have to be, we are able to listen to others from a place of presence and focus. This can be invaluable in our decision-making and in our leadership presence and direction. The Return marks an end to this cycle of inner change—for now—and is essentially a return to our Normal World, but now with even more to contribute to others in how we lead and influence. We draw from more expansive narratives in this phase of the Hero's Journey that free us from the need to push the river, to *force* changes to occur in our realm of influence. We become more comfortable with what *is* while also choosing how to bring our own gifts and influence to bear in our relationships, teams, organization, family, and community.

It's not easy, and it takes work. But the promise of the quest, of the Hero's Journey, is that as we go, we become more and more comfortable in our own skin. We get to be more of ourselves, *of who we truly are.* And we can bring more of our Whole Selves to how we lead. We become more contemplative leaders. If we currently feel dissatisfied with our leadership experiences, then perhaps we're approaching the point of a new Departure; if we feel lost or confused, then we might already be in a phase of Descent, where our whole world is becoming reordered; or, if we feel refreshed and renewed, with a new perspective on what it is we have to offer and where it is we want to contribute, then we are likely in the Return phase of the Hero's Journey.

Moving through the three phases of the Hero's Journey isn't a one-off experience. It's something that happens again and again in big and small ways throughout our lives. It applies to the personal learnings that we take from hard times and how we bring these lessons back to the people we lead and influence. As such, the Hero's Journey is a framework for change that helps us *reframe* the narratives we have inherited so that we can choose to lead from a story that we have consciously selected, one that deepens, serves, and inspires us and others.

REFLECTIVE EXERCISE

- Take a few minutes to consider your answers to the questions under the headings of ontology and epistemology on page 55.
- Broadly speaking, which phase of the Hero's Journey do you sense you are in today: Departure, Descent, or Return?
- What is your *current* ontology and epistemology within this phase?

Ontology	Epistemology
What narratives did you inherit from your family about what constituted "the good life," and what was expected of you and your future? What narratives from the following contexts have influenced the kind of leader you have become? · Your school experiences: e.g., "Learning is fun" or "Learning is not relevant for daily life" · Your local-community interactions: e.g., "Kind neighbors are crucial" or "Racism/sexism/ageism is permissible" · Society: e.g., "Service and sacrifice are a person's highest calling" or "Power and money are of utmost importance"	For each of your answers to the ontology questions, reflect on the sources that have supported the validity of your narratives: · Role models: e.g., a parent, relative, coach, teacher, famous personality, local activist, or religious leader · Books: e.g., a sacred text such as the Bible/Koran/Torah/Vedas/Buddhist sutras or a meaningful text, such as the Constitution, that represents truth to you · Videos: e.g., a movie that taught you about reality that you have returned to over and over to remind you of what's true or what's worth pursuing in life · Institutions: e.g., a police force, the Supreme Court, educational institutions, or sports clubs

Ontology	Epistemology

Chapter 3

LEADING FROM OUR BODY

Presence is a courageous act, but the only way you can get present is if you are able to resource yourself.
—Louise Chester

If we've ever comforted a crying child, we've had firsthand experience of the positive effects that our presence can have. Sometimes, the only way to calm them is to hold them tight against our chest. The vibrations of our heartbeat, the sound of our breathing, and the calm, relaxed presence of our body against theirs eventually causes them to calm down and relax, too. I remember a few 3 AM wakes, picking up my infant son as he sobbed in his crib, taking some deep breaths with him pressed against my chest. Within minutes, his heart rate would slow and his breathing would deepen and fall into sync with my own. His nervous system would return to a place of regulation after being co-regulated by mine. We would then both go back to sleep in a calm state, feeling relaxed and connected.

In this very simple but profound experience lies a fundamental lesson of polyvagal theory in action. And a working knowledge of what it is and how to modulate through our three nervous system states can be transformational to our practice of contemplative leadership.

BODY-BASED LEADERSHIP

In 1994, the behavioral neuroscientist Stephen W. Porges first presented his polyvagal theory to the Society for Psychophysiological Research in Atlanta, Georgia.[1] He proposed that there are three autonomic nervous system states that we all experience as humans. Porges's work was further developed by the researcher and psychotherapist Deb Dana, who arranged these three states in sequence, like the three rungs of a ladder that we climb up and down:

1. Ventral vagal state: the rest-and-digest state, where we feel safe and connected with ourselves and comfortable interacting with others

2. Sympathetic state: where we are mobilized and vigilant, alert for threats in our environment

3. Dorsal vagal state: where we are immobilized and in "shutdown," recovering from our experiences of the sympathetic state[2]

Each of these states has a role in protecting us and keeping us alive. But whereas some of these states are reactionary in nature, focusing primarily on our survival, others are more restorative, helping us regulate our emotions, sensations, and thoughts.

Our autonomic nervous system encompasses our bodily functions, our cognition, and our emotional states. According to polyvagal theory, we have a series of nerves that take over the dominant functioning of our nervous system in response to shifting stimuli in our environment. Our blood pressure, digestive system, various glands, heart rate, conscious thoughts, emotions, and physical sensations are all interconnected within our nervous system and can all undergo rapid changes as a response to our moment-by-moment experiences. For example, say a colleague we struggle to get along with unexpectedly walks into our office with an angry look on their face. In an instant, we shift from quietly working away, feeling comfortable and relaxed, to suddenly feeling tense with a knot in our stomach. Our breathing becomes shallow, our heart rate increases, our palms or armpits become sweaty, and we desperately rack our brain for all the potential reasons this colleague is angry and what we can say to best engage in this stressful interaction. We have just shifted from the ventral vagal state to the sympathetic state.

Nervous System State	Characteristics
Ventral vagal state (Part of the parasympathetic nervous system*)	Relaxed and safe: connection with self and others; rest-and-digest state
Sympathetic state (Part of the sympathetic nervous system)	Mobilized and vigilant for threats: fight, flight, or fawn
Dorsal vagal state (Part of the parasympathetic nervous system)	Immobilized and shut down: low energy; recovery state

---

* Although the parasympathetic nervous system state is often referred to as the rest-and-digest state, it should be noted that polyvagal theory divides it into two sections: the ventral and dorsal vagal states. We can experience, for example, a slower heart rate and relaxed muscles in both states, but whereas we'll have lower energy and sometimes feel emotionally vulnerable in the dorsal vagal state, we'll usually feel more energetic and emotionally resilient in the ventral vagal state.

The diagram on page 59 illustrates the key characteristics of each of these three states. Our lived experience of these states is unique to us and varies depending on how we're attuning to the environment we're in.

As we apply the polyvagal theory to our leadership presence, let's begin by examining all three states in some detail, reflect on our own experiences of each, and then find ways to modulate between them.

1. SYMPATHETIC STATE

Something happens in our environment that sets us on edge. In a split second, we move from being very relaxed (the vagal state) to instantly becoming vigilant and prepared for a huge amount of threat. This happens because a part of our brain called the thalamus receives information from our sense organs (eyes, ears, nose, tongue, and skin) that it in turn communicates to another part of the brain, the amygdala, which is responsible for our emotional brain functioning. The amygdala then communicates with the hippocampus, the part of the brain that stores memories of our previous experiences. And if the hippocampus confirms that this current situation is like other threatening situations that have taken place before, then the amygdala shuts down the functioning of the neocortex—the part of our brain responsible for social behaviors and rational thoughts—to prioritize the emotional brain activity of the limbic system. We move into a kind of survival state, a very focused and almost myopic nervous system state, where the brain and body's sole function becomes about surviving this current threat. The psychologist and science journalist Daniel Goleman calls this process the "amygdala hijack."[3] This can be very helpful when our level of reaction is appropriate for the level of threat. But if this is not the case—for example, if we are in an office environment, or chatting with somebody in a restaurant, or at the bar when we experience an amygdala hijack—we can sometimes overreact in ways that are disproportionate to the situation. The amygdala hijack skews our perception of the *actual* level of threat in our environment, and we can react by behaving in irrational, destructive ways.

In this state, we are vigilant, perceiving a threat in our environment. Our body releases cortisol and adrenaline (also known as norepinephrine or noradrenaline[4]), among other hormones, and our heart rate increases as the adrenaline courses its way through our body, preparing us for one of three actions: fight, flight, or fawn.

When our ancestors were still roaming the earth in nomadic bands,[5] it was common to encounter a physical threat such as a spider, a large predator, or an unexpected drop along their path. This would trigger their amygdala-hijack response, essentially shutting down much of the functioning of their neocortex. They'd have a heightened state of awareness, honing in on the perceived threats with all their senses. In that context, it was a good, healthy, and appropriate autonomic nervous system response. And it's sometimes appropriate for us to react this way as well, whenever we feel threatened by other people—be they colleagues, other leaders, or customers—or find ourselves in situations such as raised voices in a meeting, dangerous working conditions, or expectations for us to work long hours under high pressure to meet a specific goal. Not to overreact by starting a physical fight or running down the corridor to "flee" a challenging meeting, but to react in more proportionate ways, to use the flow of sympathetic nervous system state hormones to stand up for ourselves, to defend our approach, to speak our mind, to gently challenge the status quo. Although we can each display fight, flight, or fawn reactions when confronted with stressful situations, we usually have a natural, unconscious preference toward one:

- **Fight:** When we get an adrenaline rush and feel the flow of the stress hormone cortisol in our body, we are ready to attack others, to raise our voice, and to fight or argue our way out of trouble.
- **Flight:** We want to run away from threat and danger. The amygdala hijack releases hormones that give us the short-term energy to run far and fast. Rather than engage in conflict or confront challenging situations head-on, we actively remove ourselves from those stressful stimuli in our environment.
- **Fawn:** We identify who is the dominant, or "alpha," person in the group and what it is we need to do socially to fit in and appease them to survive this situation.[6] For example, do I need to laugh at a joke or agree with something that somebody says? This is a survival reaction, and it is, in many ways, a very careful and calculating way of dealing with threat. (Not all theorists list the fawn reaction as a sympathetic nervous system state response, but I've seen it so often in teams and in group interactions that I've chosen to include it here.)

When we're in this sympathetic nervous system state, we're very focused on *this moment*, not on what might happen in hours, days, weeks, months, or years to come. This state helps focus our physical and emotional resources to survive the challenges that we're currently facing.

Lots of managers and leaders have made their careers by operating from within this state. They thrive in high-pressure environments that require a hard-charging pace. They can become addicted to cortisol, almost seeking out problems or creating problems that otherwise wouldn't exist to kick into gear, get a huge amount of energy, and focus to get their way. In certain high-pressure environments, where other people are similarly high-octane and this approach to controlling one's environment is seen as helpful, it can dominate the organizational culture. Not surprisingly, I've encountered this with financial traders, but I've also seen this happen in other industries.

One coachee in tech had spent her entire career operating with this sense of urgency and vigilance synonymous with the sympathetic nervous system state. When she began to near the top level of the business, her company wanted to give her a significant leadership role. But moving from micromanaging the day-to-day of her team members to leading others from more of a bird's-eye view proved to be very challenging for her. Her default reaction was to get down into the weeds, put pressure on other people, and bring a combative approach to every interaction. When others wouldn't respond in exactly the way she wanted them to, she would complete their work herself, "so as to get it done right."

We had an interesting couple of years working together, both one-on-one and then within the overall leadership team at her organization. She slowly learned to become aware of her behavior, to notice the triggering situations that led to it, and to understand the impact this had on others. She learned about her sympathetic nervous system state and that she had a propensity to catastrophize and therefore justify her need to step in and take control. She "felt alive" when she was facing a crisis and, for her, a crisis was any time she didn't have total control of all the activities of each of her team members. Upon reflection, she later told me that, for that period in her life, she only felt like she was leading when she was responding to a crisis. So she regularly and unconsciously created crisis after crisis so she could step in and fight her way through. She was, in essence, addicted to cortisol, to the rush and impetus for action that this gave her.

The sympathetic nervous system state is good and healthy, as it helps us control our reactions to stay alive. But in contemporary leadership scenarios, it usually appears when we attempt to control our environment, to survive socially. We don't want to be laughed at, to lose face, or to be mocked; we want to look like we know what we're doing in front of our boss, our client, and our team, and so we shut down any dissenting voices or any questioning of the way forward.

But if we spend a lot of time in this state, with cortisol and adrenaline flooding our body on a regular basis, we'll eventually become depleted and burned out. And as our energy reserves become depleted, we move into our dorsal vagal nervous system state.

2. DORSAL VAGAL STATE

When the dorsal vagal state kicks in, we feel tired—we have no more capacity to deal with perceived threats and challenges in our immediate environment. We want to lay down on the couch, take the night off, or just go to bed. Our productivity diminishes. Simple tasks become extremely difficult. One day, we had all this energy to fight, to take flight, or to fawn—and then the next day, we've crashed. We might find ourselves sitting down or curling up and leaning forward in poses where we unconsciously protect our vital organs. We may even find ourselves lying in bed in the recovery position.

And it's important that we experience this state. It's our body's way of forcing us to rest and recuperate. We can't continue at the pace we were operating at before. Extended times of stress from our sympathetic nervous system state has led to us ignoring the different seasons of life, the cycles of rest and recovery that are as important to our physiology as pushing and moving at pace.

The longer and harder we run while in our sympathetic nervous system state, the more likely that our crash into the dorsal vagal state will last some time. My teenage years of pushing and working very hard in all aspects of my life led me to a deep experience of depression and chronic fatigue syndrome. I remember my doctor telling me that I didn't have clinical depression, as there was no chemical imbalance that he could detect, but that I was exhausted, I was emotionally disappointed with life, and I needed lots of rest. I had been attaching myself to certain narratives, holding on to them very tightly and trying to make them work out for too long a period.

The interesting thing that I have noticed with leaders I've worked with, in a coaching as well as in a psychotherapeutic context, is that the higher functioning they are, the greater the chance that they'll push and push against seemingly impossible odds for a very long period. Then eventually, when their resources are truly sapped, they tend to fall off a cliff, deep into the dorsal vagal state. As a society, we learned a long time ago the importance of taking a day off in the week to aid with our rest and recovery. We need recreation time to "re-create" ourselves and recharge our batteries with time away from everyday work pressures. In this dorsal vagal state, however, we can really freeze, becoming immobilized and incapacitated, literally no longer able to move.

BECOMING STUCK

The challenge for many leaders today in high-pressure environments is that we can alternate between the high pressure—the fight, flight, or fawn—of the sympathetic nervous system state and the exhaustion and incapacitation—the freeze—of the dorsal vagal state. And we repeat this pattern of being close to burnout, then crashing and resting, catching our breath again, and returning to pushing and forcing for another sprint while operating from our sympathetic nervous system state. We can repeat this cycle for short periods of time, but it is not sustainable over the long term. It will cause us to lose focus and motivation and miss the bigger picture of why we are leading. Our presence will be impacted and we will find it difficult to connect with others. It's very hard to empathize with others or to think in holistic terms when we're in this state. And what we need to do is to find ways of modulating our state to get us into our more resourceful ventral vagal state. There are many ways of doing this, but the following four approaches are a great start:

1. Sigh[7]
2. Stretch[8]
3. Smile[9]
4. Gentle touch with words[10]

CHANGING TO A MORE RESOURCEFUL NERVOUS SYSTEM STATE

1. SIGH

I once went on safari in South Africa, and we saw an impala being chased by a lion. In the end, the one impala that had become isolated from the others managed to outrun the lion. Soon afterward, while we were sitting down in our little treetop lodge, we saw this same impala come toward us and twitch beneath our balcony for a full forty minutes. It was taking short, fast breaths to start with, but these relaxed down into slow, deep breaths over the first twenty minutes or so. It continued to twitch all the muscles in its legs and back until eventually its muscles were able to relax. Then it calmly walked out from the shelter of the trees, now in a very relaxed state, back into the grass on the open plain. It had transitioned from a vigilant nervous system "flight" state to one of calm and composure.

As humans, we need to find ways of changing our state for ourselves, from high stress (sympathetic nervous system state) or low energy (dorsal vagal state) to a state of self-regulation, resourcefulness, and presence. But, unlike many animals, we don't naturally twitch to release the buildup of hormones from our body.

Whether we're aware of it or not, we all sigh quite often. And when we are sighing, it's not just a deep breath; there's an audible sound that comes with it that helps us to release tension held in our body. We need to do big sighs to relax and "let it all out." When I'm working with clients, we sigh a minimum of five times over the course of at least one minute. The louder the better. I encourage you to practice this now before moving on.

2. SMILE

The next state-changing exercise is to smile. We smile when we are happy and out of social necessity, and when we do, the muscles on our face transmit messages to our brain that we are feeling relaxed and calm. We can control the smile muscles that curve around our mouth (zygomaticus major and minor), but the muscles around our eyes (orbicularis oculi), which give us crow's feet, can only be activated when we are genuinely laughing or smiling. However, even just smiling with our mouth can have a profound effect on our state.[11] Take a moment now to hold a smile for a minimum of thirty seconds (ideally sixty seconds). And let it be, as I say to my coachees, "the biggest smile that you can make, until your face hurts." You can look out the window or look at yourself in the mirror while holding this smile. But please try it now before moving on and see if it makes any difference to how you're feeling. Continuing to sigh while holding this big smile is very helpful to practice.

3. STRETCH

Next, we want to get into some stretching. It doesn't need to be anything extreme—no lunges or large movements are required, just gentle stretches, gentle movements of the body. Many people find that rolling their shoulders, stretching their arms, hands, and fingers, or very gently stretching their neck can be very effective for this state-changing exercise.

When we stretch, our body releases blood flow to the muscle being extended. It also encourages the release of endorphins, hormones that can give us a sense of tranquility and general relaxation. Pay attention to where in your body you want to stretch; it might be the places named above or else your hips, legs, or lower back. Stretching helps to stimulate our parasympathetic nervous system, allowing us to rest and digest as well as socially engage with others from a calm place of self-regulation.[12,13] Take a few moments to stretch now and experience the benefits of this state-changing exercise. Remember to keep breathing while you stretch.

4. GENTLE TOUCH WITH WORDS

Finally, the last of our state-change exercises is a gentle touch. When we are stressed and have a lot of adrenaline and cortisol flowing through our body, we enter the survival state of our sympathetic nervous system. From here, it can be extremely difficult to enter a calmer state where there is self-compassion and empathy, where we are able to move away from a hard-charging, task-orientated, transactional focus to something that is more accepting and non-judgmental. We need to take care of ourselves before we can take care of other people. Otherwise, we will, again, just get burned out by leading, serving, giving, and expending our energy all the time. Sometimes a gentle form of touch can be what we need to re-ground ourselves.

Think about which part of your body would feel most appropriate, most natural, to experience a gentle touch. Is it your arm, your neck, your hand, or your thigh? Consider a part of your body that you can easily reach. Sometimes people find it helpful, rather than just placing their hand, to instead give a gentle rub somewhere, like their shoulder or their chest. Become aware of what kind of movement or touch would help you move away from hard-charging, pressing, and pushing toward a place of connection, safety, and relaxation.

And notice if there is a phrase that comes up for you, something that helps remind you, "This is what I need to remember about myself." For example: "You're doing well, just as you are" or "You've got all the resources that you need in this moment."

It we struggle to come up with a phrase for ourselves, it can be good to think about a message from someone else who cares for us. It might be from a mentor or from a boss who says, "You've got great presence." Make sure it's not focused on what you *do* but *who you are*. With my grandmother, I always got a sense of "You're good fun, and I love you" when I was around her. And over the years, I've returned to that sense of acceptance from her, something that I often need to experience when I struggle to hear this kind of encouraging voice from within.

Take a few moments to engage in this gentle-touch exercise now, with or without encouraging words.

REFLECT
- Having completed these four short exercises:
  - What sensations can you feel in your body?
  - What emotions are you experiencing?

Going through these four exercises helps us regularly experience a shift into the ventral vagal nervous system state. We usually feel calmer, more relaxed, or peaceful. We have self-regulated our nervous system and feel safe and reconnected with ourselves.

3. VENTRAL VAGAL STATE

The ventral vagal state produces a sense of safety and connection where we feel comfortable, functioning in a way where our brain is aligned with our body. This more easily allows us to express our creativity and see possibilities and opportunities. There are many paths that bring us to this place of self-regulation, from the four practices of sigh, stretch, smile, and touch to meditation, gentle exercise, and spending time in nature.

In addition to self-regulation, we can also co-regulate with other people and animals, where spending time with them makes us feel present and good about ourselves, alive and able to rest and digest. We can even co-regulate our nervous system when we cast our minds back to memories of loved ones who have died with whom we have positive associations. Just remembering what it was like to be with them, how we felt about ourselves when we were in their company, is all that might be required to return us to a state of calm and tranquility.

Co-regulating others through our very presence is one of the greatest gifts we can give, especially to people who look to us for leadership. We can make others feel seen, known, respected, and even present to themselves. Our ventral vagal state can bring a sense of hope and confidence to others even without saying a word.

A few years ago, I was running an in-house mentoring program for middle managers, and, as part of the mentor training, we were purposefully noticing the effect of these different states on another person in conversation. At one point, through my body language, tone of voice, and sparse use of verbal communication, I made one of the mentors feel quite uncomfortable. I didn't make eye contact, my facial expression conveyed disinterest in his story, and I occasionally checked my watch as if looking for our conversation to soon be over. Within one minute of our interaction, he was on edge; he stopped telling me about his work scenario and told me how "very uncomfortable" he felt. A few minutes later, I exhibited a completely different set of body language, tone of voice, and verbal communication, and he relaxed and opened up, filling me in on all the details of his story. I nodded along with him, saying, "Mm-hmm" and, "Aha" and, "Oh, really?" as he explained the challenging scenario he was facing. I asked some open-ended questions, starting with the questions "What?" and "How?"—giving him time and scope to really consider his answers. "That was so different," he said at the end. "I went from being defensive and not saying much to really feeling that you were with me in it. And that I could find a way through it."

"What was the difference?" I asked.

"I just felt more . . . comfortable."

When we interact with others while we are in a ventral vagal nervous system state, our sense of calm and relaxation, interest, and empathy shine through. We extend an invitation to others to co-regulate with us.

The ventral vagal state is the easiest nervous system state in which to be nonattached, to truly be contemplative. We don't feel threatened, pressured, or forceful about outcomes; we can bring a sense of play, creativity, and curiosity that leads to deeper intrapersonal awareness and interpersonal connection. It's an extremely resourceful state from which to lead.

The last thing I say to colleagues before we facilitate a leadership program together, after lots of detailed training, is, "We've learned all the steps, tips, and best approaches. Now we can forget about them. What's even *more* important is that we are present. Create the space for the people in our group, allow them to show up any way they want, give them a voice, and encourage them to *be* and to *speak* by your very presence." It's an invitation to self-regulate so that we can co-regulate with others. And I say this to my colleagues as a way of reminding myself that my presence is the greatest leadership I can bring to others.

HOW TO REGULARLY ACCESS THE VENTRAL VAGAL STATE

Gaining greater personal awareness and practicing new behaviors that reinforce this awareness are two essential steps for meaningful change to occur. The following four exercises, when practiced, facilitate changes in our awareness and behaviors that allow us to regularly engage with life from our ventral vagal nervous system state.

1. PLACES

Think about the places you go to in your daily life, or that you can go to in general, that help you access a state of safety and connection. It could be your bedroom, a park, a garden, a coffee shop, your porch, the lakeshore, or the ocean.

- What are the physical spaces and places you love going to that make you feel calm and relaxed? Go there more regularly.

2. PEOPLE

Who are the people that, when you're around them, help you feel comfortable and present to yourself as well as to them? Some of us are in social circles because we want to belong there, but we may not feel *at ease* there. Think about the people that make you feel most relaxed, most yourself. It might be someone in your personal life or someone at work—a mentor, a guide, a colleague, a friend, a partner, a child. It can even be an animal you love or the memory of a loved one who is no longer around. Not everyone is fortunate enough to have somebody like this in their life. But if you do, try to spend more time with this person. Co-regulating your nervous system with them will give you a more stable base from which to lead and influence in every aspect of your life.

- Who will you purposefully spend more time with, on a daily, weekly, or monthly basis, whose presence will help you access your ventral vagal state?

3. TIMES

At which times of the day is it easier for you to access this state of presence and connection? Are you a morning lark, a night owl, or something in between? Personally, I'm a night owl. Sometimes, if I'm in a country where the weather is warm, I'll start work at eleven or twelve at night. As I sit under the stars, in the quiet, my thinking becomes clearer. Other people prefer the hustle and bustle of the middle of the day when the light and the general activity of others energizes them. I know others who are morning larks, who prefer the quiet of early morning and who get up before everyone else at 5 AM to have some high-quality time of focus.

- Notice at which times in your day that it's easiest for you to access your ventral vagal state. Adjust your daily schedule, even just for a week, to more fully experience these times in your day that make you feel relaxed and present to yourself.
- When in the year do you feel most relaxed and comfortable—during vacations, on certain holidays, when celebrating birthdays, when it's cold and snowy, or when the colors of fall make you catch your breath? Look at old photos of enjoyable moments and notice the emotions and the physical sensations you feel in your body as you relive those beautiful experiences.

4. ACTIVITIES

What are the situations and activities that help you to get into this ventral vagal state? Is it when you're brainstorming with colleagues? Playing sports? Is it when you are being playful with your child?

Or taking a bath or shower? Is it when you are walking, reading, or listening to music? Gardening, cleaning, cooking, driving, serving others, or listening to and talking with others?

For years, I have gone for very gentle swims in the pool at the quietest times of day, either mid-morning or late in the evening. I gather myself, relax from the busyness of life, and think through challenges I am facing in work. The lapping of the water and the gentle movement of my body allow me to enter this ventral vagal state and think differently about life. I continue to regularly find myself staring out the window at the distant clouds, my arms resting on the pool wall, sighing deeply as I process the latest insights that come to me from beneath the water.

- What are some of the activities that allow you to feel relaxed and to think clearly?

A TIME FOR ALL THREE STATES

There is a time and a place for us to lead from each of these three states. When we are in our sympathetic nervous system state, we tend to lead in a transactional way, often focusing on tasks and getting things done. There are many scenarios where this is very appropriate, when we're focused and efficiently getting through challenges that we must deal with urgently. But the challenge for many leaders is that this is the dominant worldview and the dominant nervous system state that we engage in, which limits our capacity to think globally, to meaningfully connect with others and draw out the best in everyone. As we move from a healthy level of focus and determination (eustress) to an unhealthy level of stress (distress), there can be a combative undertone to our interactions and relationships. This can work in the short term, but it usually leads to challenging work-place environments over the medium to long term.

REFLECTIVE EXERCISES

1. Answer the following questions for each of the three nervous system states outlined in this chapter:*, [14]

Sympathetic State	1.	What's physically happening in your body while in this state?
	2.	What kinds of thoughts do you have?
	3.	What kinds of emotions do you have?
	4.	What presence and sense of inner awareness do you experience?
	5.	What's the quality of your connection with and behavior toward others?
	6.	"When I'm in this state, life seems . . ."
Dorsal Vagal State	1.	What's physically happening in your body while in this state?
	2.	What kinds of thoughts do you have?
	3.	What kinds of emotions do you have?
	4.	What presence and sense of inner awareness do you experience?
	5.	What's the quality of your connection with and behavior toward others?
	6.	"When I'm in this state, life seems . . ."

---

* The ordering of the three states in this exercise, starting with sympathetic, moving to dorsal, and then finishing with the ventral vagal state, is adapted from an exercise I experienced while completing a training course with Deb Dana.

Ventral Vagal State	1.	What's physically happening in your body while in this state?
	2.	What kinds of thoughts do you have?
	3.	What kinds of emotions do you have?
	4.	What presence and sense of inner awareness do you experience?
	5.	What's the quality of your connection with and behavior toward others?
	6.	"When I'm in this state, life seems . . ."

2. List the elements that help you engage with your ventral vagal state:[15]

Places?	People?
Times?	Activities?

3. What leadership situations, conversations, decisions, strategizing, solo work, one-to-one meetings, and so on elicit each of the three states for you? Write these out in the table on page 77.

4. Consider the four state-change exercises we examined (sigh, stretch, smile, and gentle touch), as well as other calming activities that you could do. What's the best way of preparing your nervous system for the leadership situations you face?

5. Reflecting on nonattachment, being present to the moment and aware of yourself and connected to others, what simple, actionable steps do you intuitively know will help you be more contemplative and less attached to outcomes in your leadership?

6. Return to the end of chapter one (page 29) and try the guided contemplative sit again. Notice what this does to your nervous system state.

Leadership situations:	The state that this generally elicits (ventral, sympathetic, or dorsal):
· Leadership conversations · Decision-making · Strategizing · Solo work · One-to-one meetings Other situations: · · · · ·	

Chapter 4

CHALLENGE AND FAILURE

Pleasant experiences make life delightful, painful experiences lead to growth.
—Tony De Mello[1]

G rowing up, Ben Keesey loved math, and, combined with a deep sense of confidence engendered by his youth group, he believed that he could make a big change in the world for good. Toward the end of college, he watched a documentary that some of his friends had made about child soldiers in Africa and simply asked himself, "What can I do to help?" Before he knew it, he was flying to Uganda to spend two months living in an active conflict zone, documenting the lives of the children and families affected by violent conflict. Traveling around with three other people, he stayed in the villages with the locals, and he remembers waking up every morning with a sense of gratitude that they'd made it through another night without their village being attacked.

Up to that point, Ben had been working summers at JPMorgan and had just committed to join the professional services firm Deloitte. But Uganda had a profound effect on him. He deferred his new role for a year and helped start the NGO Invisible Children from a documentary project into a nonprofit organization. As chief financial officer, he built the accounting and HR system, got legal compliance, and then oversaw the fundraising of $300,000 in the organization's first year. "There was incredible momentum right away," he says. "We were bringing high-level attention to a neglected crisis. We were invited to premieres in LA; big celebrities were getting involved and supporting our work. We were presenting at events in New York and DC. There was an intoxication to that—it was both meaningful and fun."

Thinking about his own approach to the work, Ben confesses, "I wanted to do well. I worked almost nonstop. Given the impact and success we were having, there was just a mountain of 'the next thing to do'—I'd boarded a rocket ship and I was holding on."

Success for this startup involved screenings of their documentary films and inviting people to donate or volunteer. They started funding former child soldiers to go to school in Uganda. And then they began to get the attention of policymakers. The organization had launched in 2005, and by 2007 they were at meetings at the White House around the anti-AIDS initiatives of the Bush administration. That same year, Ben transitioned from the role of CFO to CEO. At the age of twenty-four, he was, as he admits, "put into the role before I was ready. I was running a $2 million-a-year nonprofit organization, just trying to do my best. I leaned on just enough leadership training I'd received from playing sports to be a fairly effective leader."

By 2010, Ben and the founders were signing a bill with President Obama in the Oval Office. 2011 saw the unprecedented deployment of US military advisors to Uganda to help track down Joseph Kony, the leader of the militia that was brutally forcing children to become soldiers. In 2011, they raised $14 million, and in the following year they launched their thirty-minute documentary, *Kony 2012*. It raised $20 million in one week and had 100 million views over six days. Then disaster struck.

One of the founders had a very public breakdown. And suddenly, in front of national and international media, the organization received wave after wave of criticism. Ben became privately overwhelmed: "'I don't know if I can do this,' I thought. 'We may not make it through this, and I don't know who I am if I'm not the CEO of Invisible Children, and I *definitely* don't know who I am if I'm the CEO of a project that fails. If this project doesn't succeed and I go through a public leadership failure, it would feel like dying. I'd have to pack up shop and call it a day because I'd no longer be a respected leader; then what would be the point?' And that's when my inner journey started, in 2013, after our road peaked and then crashed."

By his own admission, Ben spent a year driven by unconscious fear. He explains,

> *If I could have had a more mature consciousness, more contemplative consciousness, then everything wouldn't have been so binary, either success or failure—where success equals "I am worthy as a leader" and failure equals "I am not"; if this organization succeeds, this is a direct reflection on me, and if this organization fails, this is a direct reflection on me. I believed strongly in the impact and importance of our work, but it was also deeper than that. My identity was attached to the outcomes; it wasn't just the effort, the intention, the process—it was the end result. We had so many successful results, we kept putting out goals and hitting them, so the idea that we could miss . . . I was hyper-attached to the outcome . . . I wish that I could have just seen it with so much more "both/and" at the time. I wish I could have seen it in the way*

I look at leaders now, leaders who go through projects that don't reach the mountaintop. But I was so binary: "If we lose, I lose."

Ben spent a year in hyper overwork, trying to double down on what had worked to get him out of tough situations in the past. "[I] was trying to grasp for control—that's what I'd been doing before, when things were going well. When I'd connect with my fear and weakness, it was always a very solo thing. Being angry that my team didn't work as hard as I did—starting to turn on the other leaders who were trying to have a more balanced and healthy life. I could get stuck in a childish mindset . . . 'All of you, people on the team, you don't care about me because you're not working as hard as me.'"

One day, Ben snapped and yelled at a key supporter: "She knew me long enough to know this wasn't really me. 'Ben,' she said, 'this is really out of character. It seems like you're not doing so well. Your year has been so intense; your founder has had a mental health crisis. Are you okay?' 'No, I'm really not okay.'" She offered to pay for an executive coach who helped Ben eventually turn a corner.

"He made the case that a lot of what was going on in my leadership had to do with my fear, and that fear had much more to do with my internal landscape than with the business," says Ben. "Fear was 'a very bad counsellor,' and I was caught in a lot of it.

"It was really beginner therapy, with him asking me questions: 'Ben, I don't want you to give me the right answer; I want you to give me the answer that's real to you.' It was really difficult. I was so used to giving people what I thought they wanted from me."

He started asking himself, for the first time, how he was actually feeling. What was his fear? He started to verbalize this idea that "if Invisible Children fails, then *I'm a failure*." His coach helped him say this out loud. And then the fear started to recede. His coach would tell him stories of other business leaders who'd been through failures. And these helped Ben "normalize the pain and the challenge."

He started reading some books, including Dan Baker's *What Happy People Know* and *Everything Belongs* by Richard Rohr. These helped him realize that he had "a lot of programming I needed to unwind to become a happier, at peace, more content person."

Originally, Ben thought that his dominant motivation for operating in the world was to be a kind of "peacemaker" in different social environments. "But that can be an external facade. Internally," he reflects, he was "more of an 'achiever.' I sought to be a chameleon personality, to match the hopes and expectations of the room in front of me. It helped me fundraise and make a huge number of connections, but internally it was very isolating. At that time, the only way I could turn off that part of my personality was to have a lot of alone time. My phone had to be turned off. Then there was nobody to impress."

Change came slowly for Ben. Amidst a very challenging work environment, he started noticing subtle shifts in his thinking throughout 2014. But Invisible Children was in decline, its budget dropping from $20 million in 2012 to $6 million in 2013 to $4 million in 2014. The narrative of personal "failure" was hard to turn down every day in the context of dwindling finances and letting go of more and more people. Soon, they were down to only five staff in the United States and their last million dollars.

"Once I stepped down and got out of the overwhelming day-to-day responsibility, that's when I started making progress," says Ben. "For eighteen months, I was doing consulting and working on myself as much as possible. We were burning through our personal savings, and I was reading a lot and learning to surf. And it was those experiences, of surfing especially, that helped—because in surfing, you have to fail in public. There's no practice in private so you don't embarrass yourself. Surfing was something I'd always wanted to do. And I did it every day for that year and confronted so many fears and insecurities because I was a total beginner!"

Ben started "untangling a lot of preconditioning of what's good, moral, and upstanding," which helped him begin to detach from his identity as a "good person" to his identity simply as a person. "That was a huge shift that allowed me to start expressing my own real thoughts, feelings, and emotions."

Ben continued surfing, going to coaching, and having hard conversations with people, and he went off social media and the speaker's circuit. "My public antennae were so developed and my internal antennae were so underdeveloped that I really needed to turn down my public ones before I could hear the internal ones.

"If you'd met me back in 2012, you'd have seen a similar person: calm, cool, and collected. But I was very different on the inside. Now I'm showing up a lot of the same ways, but the internal landscape is much less 'closed fist' control, worry about outcomes, and it's much more 'trust that I'm just kind of floating down the river of life.' It's much less attached to outcomes, and it's much more comfortable with—and I still don't like it—but much more comfortable with disappointing people, of not worrying that I'm hitting the A+ of their expectations for me," says Ben.

In addition to becoming less attached to outcomes, Ben is now more aware of himself and the presence he brings to each interaction. "Something I've heard from someone since [is that], in leading a growing business, my work on myself was as important an ingredient as my work and leadership on the business. My fear of failure was a big ingredient in manifesting what I didn't want; my attempt to control post-*Kony 2012* was connected with our inability to do it," he explains. "If I could have been a lot more free and creative in that time, not controlled by unconscious fear, I could have had a better chance at creating an outcome that we wanted at the time."

One of the key factors in moving from reactive fear to leading with a sense of freedom and creativity is to cultivate self-compassion. This involves becoming aware of our inner workings, acknowledging our capabilities while accepting our shortcomings. Then we're better able to be kind and compassionate to ourselves.

"If I could go back in time, I would say to myself, 'Ben, you'll get through this and a) in hindsight, you won't even think of this as failure, and b) if it [ends up] a failure, you'll get through that, too.' This path has paid dividends in my own life, my own ability to stay grounded, be content, remain kind—but sincerely kind, not just 'performance kind'—in the face of challenges."

Reflecting on the practices and activities that help maintain this more contemplative approach to leading and dealing with failure, Ben says, "Surfing is a great indicator; how I feel now out on the board in the water is just so different. That's a practice. I know how it used to feel paddling out, [and] I know how it feels now. I'm excited, I'm happy to be there! It feels like I'm going to enjoy this next hour. I'm not doing this for training, to 'not embarrass myself,' to survive while looking good—I'm out here to enjoy life while doing this amazing thing . . . As opposed to only seeing it as an exercise in getting better so that the people watching me won't think that I don't know what I'm doing. And that gives me a lot of inner confidence that this is the right path . . . I recognize it mostly when I see contentment in older people—that makes me think, 'I want to follow that path.'"

SITTING WITH CHALLENGE AND FAILURE

Departure from the Normal World of business as usual, of winning and success, and opening ourselves up to the possibility of personal change is a challenging experience. It can feel very painful on an emotional, psychological, and even physical level. The traditional narrative of the Western worldview over the past few centuries, certainly since the time of the Enlightenment, has been all about progress and changing things for the better. We expect exponential personal development and hockey-stick growth curves for our organizations. But this kind of growth is not the lived experience of most people. For many of us, however, growing up, we were taught to hide our failures and not focus on the learnings of challenges—to quickly pick ourselves up, suppress uncomfortable emotions, and move on without learning the lessons of what our difficult times can teach us.

Ben's story reminds us of the nature of failure and our understanding of what our experience of failure says about us. Failure is extremely subjective and is more influenced by our context and the narrative we ascribe to the failure situation than by whatever outcome was not achieved.

For some of us, a B grade in our studies feels like the end of the world. For others, that's fantastic. Something similar happens in work; we get a 5 percent bonus, and because of what we're expecting—what we've received in the past or what our partner, friends, or colleagues have received—it feels like a disaster. But others might have only been expecting 1 or 2 percent, so receiving 5 percent is an amazing outcome. An interesting way of exploring the narratives we have around failure and disappointment is to reflect on the inner mindset that influences how we experience challenge.

"Growth mindset" and "fixed mindset" are the two terms coined by psychology researcher Carol Dweck to explain how the narrative we have around effort and failure affects our motivation and behavior. Her famous 2006 book, *Mindset*, includes a chapter on the growth and fixed mindsets of various leaders.

With a growth mindset, we approach things with a playful attitude, an openness of mind, a sense of "Let's just see what I can learn, how I can grow." When this is the starting point of our mindset, there's no such thing as failure; we're just learning which strategies work, and we expect there to be many learning experiences along the way until we find an approach that gives us what we're looking for. With a fixed mindset, however, we are very attached to outcomes. We're not focused on the process, the learnings of failures and setbacks, or to easily adapting our approaches as we go. We feel we have to achieve certain results.

In one study, Dweck and her colleagues first asked participants to complete a short questionnaire that showed if they had a fixed or growth mindset.[2] They then gave them a test of common-knowledge questions (e.g., "What's the capital of Australia?"), and each time they got a question wrong, they saw what the right answer was. Then, unexpectedly for the participant, once they had completed all the questions, they were immediately asked to take the same test a second time. The participants were connected to functional magnetic resonance imaging (fMRI) so Dweck and her colleagues could see their brain activity throughout both rounds of the test.

Participants with a growth mindset had "externally focused brains" that were able to "regulate sensory and response selection."[3] They were curious to find out what the correct answers were to any questions they got wrong the first time around and were pretty good at learning and filling them in during round two of the test.[4] Those with a fixed mindset, however, didn't do as well the second time around. They had more brain activity in the part of their limbic system that regulates internal emotional responses.[5] When they got an answer wrong, more of their brain activity was taken up by regulating their internal emotional response rather than learning something new. Their negative feedback was seen as "a threat to self-perception about ability rather than as a challenge to improve."[6] A fixed-mindset approach to leadership is results-oriented and very much about pass or fail, a zero-sum game. Fixed-mindset leaders value outcomes and can focus much of their energy on making sure that they don't lose, that they don't perform any worse than they did before. They are more interested in maintaining their past record. This means that the pressure is on to defend their position rather than to learn something new from what is happening.

Dweck and her colleagues discovered that when people with fixed mindsets are problem-solving, they might only make one or two attempts to overcome a challenge. Those with a growth mindset will instead make multiple attempts to overcome a challenge until they find an approach that works. With a fixed mindset, we think, *It's too hard; I can't do it*, and we bow out of difficult tasks. With a growth mindset, we bring a sense of curiosity, openness, and playfulness that causes us to ask, *How else can I approach this?*

We know from other research that our brains are neuroplastic, meaning they can rewire themselves again and again.[7] Our thinking can change, our approach to situations can develop, and we can constantly learn and grow throughout our lives if we have the mindset that facilitates this playful trial-and-error approach to learning. So what does it mean to lead in a contemplative way as we approach challenge and failure?

MINDSET, CHALLENGE, AND CONTEMPLATIVE LEADERSHIP

As leaders, we need to stop framing whatever we're doing as an all-or-nothing scenario. We need to correctly frame the context, saying to ourselves, *I'm going to do the best that I can. I'm going to follow up each unsuccessful attempt by tweaking the process, asking some questions, learning from others—and then I'll go through the next round of trial and error. We'll see what happens next. And if I find myself reacting to failure with a fight, flight, or fawn response, I can be self-compassionate, listen to my fears, and patiently find ways to change my autonomic nervous system state.* This kind of nonattachment and leading from this place requires a lifetime of practice. It takes time to move away from the fixed-mindset approach of being attached to outcomes, of being predominantly motivated by fear and a desire to emotionally self-regulate while in a sympathetic nervous system state.

Embracing the growth mindset, shifting our focus from merely surviving the shame of failure to being focused on learning and developing, requires a nonattachment to outcomes. Instead of on outcomes, we focus on being present to ourselves, others, and to *this* situation, *this* moment—to working hard, being flexible, and changing our strategies and approaches along the way. Our brain functioning changes, and our whole nervous system operates from our ventral vagal state, enabling us to engage in the world with a more curious, open presence.

Ben, by his own admission, initially doubled down and worked harder than ever when things started to go wrong at Invisible Children. But his thinking remained the same—his focus on outcomes over processes caught him in a bind, where so much of his effort was related to saving face as a leader. As is the case for many leaders, it often takes a significant crisis that we can't overcome through our normal approaches that forces us to take an honest look at ourselves.

THE POWER OF "SHOULD"

In my coaching, therapy, and consulting work, I often hear leaders use the word "should." It's a classic word to look out for in the helping professions. Using words like "should" often reveals there is an objective narrative at play, a particular reality that is the "truth" and that must be adhered to. For example, "I *should* get a promotion within two years," "My team *should* know what I want by now," or "We *should* have more customers by this point in our startup process." Thinking in "shoulds" is a surefire way of regularly operating from within our sympathetic nervous system state, as we remain highly vigilant, checking that each milestone of our master plan is turning out exactly as we'd like.

A lot of the time, I'm asked to coach people because they have certain "shoulds" that are nonnegotiable. There's little flexibility around how they, their team, and their department "should" be. This brings a lot of pressure and frustration. Their performance becomes restricted, their focus narrows, they lose energy, and they cannot see alternatives to the realities they are facing.

These "shoulds" reflect our ontology, the inherent narrative of how our lives are "supposed" to be. The people we've been exposed to and the stories that have most shaped our choices all play a key part in this narrative. I often refer to it as "the script." Typical examples of the script include: "I'll travel the world for two years, then do my MBA, spend three years in Silicon Valley, decide which country to live in next, and be headhunted for an exec role" or, "By twenty-eight, I'll buy a house; by thirty, I'll be married; by thirty-five, I'll be a parent to three kids." With leaders and founders of companies I've worked with, the script can go something like this: "First, I'm going to gain two years of experience in that company, then I'll wait for the stock options to accumulate and either leave or hopefully get a package and go on 'gardening leave.' Then I'll start a new company with seed fundraising from my network, and we'll have series funding rounds A and B within five years before series C and an IPO by year ten."

It's good to have a vision and a general outline of a plan for achieving our goals. But when we become *attached* to these visions and plans, to the script, then we start to compare that script against our lived reality. And if we're not ticking off each item at the right time, then we can feel the pressure. We start to think things like *I should be moving internationally this year* or *We should have received series funding by now* or *Why am I not being headhunted for exec roles? It's happening to other MBA alumni; it should have happened already for me.*

When our list of "shoulds" escalates to this extent, it can be very difficult to know how to come back to the experiences of here and now. It can be hard to remember—or even to imagine—what it was like to live without an overwhelming sense of what we should be doing or achieving but aren't. Part of this has to do with shame and guilt.

SHAME AND GUILT

Feeling guilt is about feeling bad about what we've done (or not done). There's a helpful guilt that makes us not want to repeat behaviors that are unhealthy for us and for our community. But feeling shame is about feeling bad for *who we are*, the kind of person we are at our core. Feeling shame has to do with the narrative of *who we should be*—of who our family and friends, our grad-school professor, our board, others in our organization, and society told us we should be.

Author and research professor at the University of Houston Brené Brown, who has spent two decades studying courage, vulnerability, shame, and empathy, talks about the two key messages of shame. Firstly, shame claims that "You're not good enough."[8] We can spend our lives, our careers, our relationships trying to prove that we are good enough and not get very far at all. Depending on our personality, the "You're not good enough" message has a different flavor and nuance as it combines with the other narratives we unconsciously believe about ourselves. But maybe after some soul-searching, we are eventually able to move beyond this limiting messaging that we're "not good enough." At that point, according to Brown, shame asks us the accusatory question, "Who do you think you are?"[9]

The only way that we can move through and beyond this double-edged sword of shame is to revisit our narratives, our script, with deep empathy. According to Brown's research, "Empathy is the antidote to shame."[10]

TIMELINE EXERCISE

What are the "shoulds" that have impacted the decisions you have made and the leader you have become?

1. Draw a timeline of your life and mark down all of the decisions you've made that have influenced the leader you've become: e.g., going to school and college, taking your first job, leading your first team/company, setting up your own venture, etc. These were not things that *happened to you*; they were decisions that *you made*.

   Here's my own example:

SIGNIFICANT DECISIONS I MADE

Age:

12 13 15 18 21 23 25 26 30 34 36

◄─┼─┼─┼─┼┼┼─┼┼─┼──┼───────────►

12: Asked my parents to send me to a different middle and high school than what they had planned for me.

13: Chose to study German in school, as it would be "practical."

15: Chose to study economics, as it would be "practical."

18: Chose to study international commerce in college, as it would be "practical."

21: Turned down the chance to work at a top investment bank in London and instead took a gap year and volunteered with a charity.

23: Took a job in management consulting, as it "made more sense as a base" for my future career.

25: Pursued my all-time dream of flying and was rejected on medical grounds.

26: Started six years of part-time study, ranging from a masters in guidance and counseling to executive and leadership coaching to theology and psychotherapy.

30: Lost a job, then turned down what would have been a big promotion elsewhere to start my company.

34: Took on employees and external consultants to widen my company's range of offerings.

36: Started to wind down those non-core business offerings that were being completed by external consultants.

Complete your own timeline:

SIGNIFICANT DECISIONS I MADE
Age:

⟵────────────────────────────────────⟶

2. Now draw a second line beneath that and, using the exact same timescale, mark out the things you most deeply wanted for yourself at those same points in time. The first timeline records the decisions you made, and the second records the things you most cared about.

Here's my example:

WHAT I REALLY WANTED
Age:
    12 13 15 18 21 23 25 26 30 34 36
⟵──┼─┼──┼──┼──┼─┼┼─┼──┼──┼──┼──⟶

12: Was delighted to attend my new school; it felt like a good fit for me. My gut instinct had been right.

13: Really wanted to study Ancient Greek instead of German; it seemed so interesting. But I was fearful that it wouldn't help my future career.

15: Really wanted to study classics instead of economics. But, again, I was fearful that it wouldn't help me in the future.

18: Really wanted to study liberal arts instead of international commerce, but—yet again—I was too scared to choose it in case it would jeopardize my future career. My deeper desire was to join the Air Force . . . but doing that before getting a primary degree would be simply unacceptable to my family.

21: Would have much preferred to dedicate that year to writing or training as a teacher or coach.

23: By this point, really would have preferred to work as a teacher.

25: Really wanted to fly and was bitterly disappointed it didn't work out. I started teaching instead.

26: Was interested in all these studies and found the theology and executive coaching particularly interesting, but there was a part of me still choosing some of these studies from a place of fear, just in case I needed additional careers to fall back on.

30: Deeply cared about starting my own company, something I believed in, that I could put my own stamp onto. It was a frightening but exhilarating time, stepping out into the unknown.

34: Really wanted to build the business more organically, but I listened to friends who encouraged me to "grow more rapidly." It became very stressful very quickly.

36: It came as a deep relief to finally choose not to maximize revenues but instead to do the work I really cared about and felt most vocational to me: coaching, writing, consulting, and training for and then practicing psychotherapy one day a week. I felt like I was contributing to different people and organizations in ways that were much more aligned with my values.

Complete your own timeline:

WHAT I REALLY WANTED

Age:

◀──▶

3. Now notice if any of your decisions were contrary to what you deeply wanted.
4. Highlight any of these scenarios that were due to a sense of "should," feeling like you had to choose something even though you didn't really want to.
5. Drawing on polyvagal theory, what kind of nervous system state were you in while making each of these decisions? Notice any patterns in decisions and states that emerge across your timeline.

Attached ◀────────────────────────▶ Detached

◆

Non-attached

6. Thinking about the words "attached," "detached," and "nonattached"—to what degree are you currently attached to or detached from the script you have for yourself, whether written by you or others?
7. What unhelpful individual scripts or general narratives do you need to move away from?

8. What empowering, more resourceful narratives will enable you to be more nonattached?

RELATING OUR SCRIPT TO CONTEMPLATIVE LEADERSHIP

Some of you reading this book may be realizing that you've been unconsciously attached to many narratives and scripts that guide your everyday choices and affect the quality of the leadership presence you embody. Perhaps you've read other leadership books and are looking out for the next set of *things I should do* or tips for *how I should lead.* But looking to these external sources for guidance distracts us from connecting with what we really want and who we really are. And as we reflect now, we're slowly deconstructing the influences that have shaped our leadership. My hope is that we can become more consciously aware of ourselves and that we can make decisions, lead, and influence from a place of personal awareness and presence.

Engaging in contemplative practices, such as the formal practice of meditation at the end of chapter two, helps our brains to rewire. As we practice, we experience a densification of neurons in the prefrontal lobe part of our neocortex.[11] The amygdala hijack doesn't take place quite as easily.[12] We therefore don't jump as quickly into our sympathetic nervous system state during times of challenge. With continued practice, over time the narratives of failure don't affect us quite as much as before.

Regular practice helps us develop the capacity to notice our stress responses in real time and examine them for a few seconds, asking questions like, "Is this interpretation of events true? Is this accurately reflecting a narrative of learning, possibility, and creativity, a narrative that serves me? Are there other ways of looking at this situation, other perspectives on what this could mean?" And since our amygdala hijack doesn't take place as quickly as it once did, we now have a little bit more time to reflect on this story we have for ourselves and the narratives we have inherited from our formative experiences and the culture of our organization or industry that tell us how we should lead, what we should do, or how we should be.

As Viktor Frankl said, "Between stimulus and response is a space, and in that space is our freedom to choose."[13] We can choose to reframe failure as an experience that is both disappointing *and* an opportunity for growth.

We learn over time how to hold a paradoxical view of reality. We learn that when you force change, it doesn't happen; getting out of the way is what allows it to happen. We can have clarity in what we want and aim for it, but we can also hold on to things a bit more loosely so that if they don't go as we hope, we can adapt. We don't have to force, we don't have to direct, we don't have to coerce. We don't have to become emotionally destabilized and mobilized, aggressive and irrational, or difficult to interact with. We can maintain some degree of calm presence as we go through challenging, difficult experiences.

Chapter 5

VALUES AND CHANGE

Your beliefs become your thoughts. Your thoughts become your words. Your words become your actions. Your actions become your habits. Your habits become your values.

Your values become your destiny.
—Mohandas Karamchand Gandhi[1]

S everal years ago, I met Matthew McCarthy at a leadership training event in London. I was struck by his humility, his approachability, and his curiosity to learn. An avid musician, on the last night of the event, he cranked out some tunes on the guitar for us to sing along to, even taking the time to teach me a blues scale. A few years later, I saw that Matthew had been appointed CEO of the Ben & Jerry's ice cream company. I was thrilled for him and delightedly read his online posts, the rationale behind his decisions and approaches to leadership. So, when I thought about a business leader who has reflected on how their values affect their leadership and, in turn, how this impacts their company, Matthew was the first person that came to mind.

"I think that joy and awe are some of the most incredible gifts that we have as humans, and I'm not sure where they come from," says Matthew. "It's amazing . . . any human, from any point in history, could be walking on a path in the woods just before daybreak and come over a crest of the hill and see the sun come up, and they feel a sense of all earthly awe . . . the older I get, the more I try to give myself the freedom to allow that kind of child in me to be part of all the things that I do. I want to show people that joy links really closely with fairness—something I value deeply.

"I kind of spent a good part of my early life figuring out my relationship to power and authority, the milieu in which we come together as people to do stuff," he says. "Fairness has been a huge driver for me in my whole life, and when things felt unfair to me or when I see people being treated unfairly, that really drives me nuts."

While in high school, Matthew worked summers and winter breaks in his dad's printing company in Massachusetts, operating the presses, cleaning floors and bathrooms, making deliveries, and learning about the ins and outs of business. He loved every minute of it, and his deep sense of curiosity kept him grounded and focused as he worked with employees and customers alike:

That's another thing that goes to fairness, to have a conversation with pretty much anybody without ego or status getting in the way. I feel much more at home chatting with people over a cold beer than I do putting on my tux and drinking champagne. I happen to have long hair and a beard, and I don't dress particularly fancy. I'll walk into a room, and people treat me one way. And then when someone says, "Oh, have you met Matthew? He's the CEO of Ben & Jerry's," everything changes. I have literally had people say to me, "No, you can't be . . . you look too normal." And this links to the main reason I went into branding; it's because I am ceaselessly interested in why we humans do the things we do.

I find it fascinating to watch human behavior when it comes to choices, interactions with others, and our relationship to "stuff." You know, that's what branding really is, people's relationship to "stuff" [that] has symbolic value, intrinsic value, and exchange value . . . how we ascribe meaning to "stuff" drives so much of how we all behave.

Matthew's curiosity and value of fairness, combined with a compassion for people, has recently led him to champion racial equity at Ben & Jerry's:

I spent most of my life as a white guy here in the States with so much privilege that I didn't really recognize . . . until later in life. In hindsight, this is probably one of the key reasons why I ended up at Ben & Jerry's. Much of what Ben & Jerry's social mission is about is fighting for people who are marginalized . . . Over the past few years within the company, we've put ourselves and the business on a new path when it comes to racial equity. I've come to believe racial equity and inclusion is the stuff of leadership, not a separate domain as I once thought. The question is, are you going to educate yourself, and are you going to do something? Are you gonna live in misguided defiance as a white person, or are you going to get on board? For me, the work that we've been doing, I thought it was going to be about civil rights and learning about how to be anti-racist. It is, and it is also about this concept of inclusion.

Inclusion is at the heart of our business model. We are absolutely in the business of serving people, and the degree to which people are not able equally to be part of our business or part of the benefits of our business—that's not only wrong, that's bad for our business. It's actually quite simple. It may not be easy, but it's very simple. To participate in the benefits of our business, you'll need a certain amount of money and access to own one of our scoop shops, or to become one of our suppliers. But not everybody has this kind of access; we don't always make our businesses fully inclusive.

Doing it the way we've always done it is a challenge to inclusion. We talk about the tug-of-war of short-term profits and short-term sales, saying, "Yeah, we just got to do this; we've always done it like this. This is our business model." But we have to stop and ask: Who are we excluding from our business model?

There are probably thousands of people that we at Ben & Jerry's have excluded from our vision of Linked Prosperity:* they couldn't get a job with us; they couldn't be a supplier to us; they couldn't be a partner to us; they couldn't be a franchisee for a variety of reasons. I believe that the purest form of business, or commerce, is one where all inequities have been eliminated. We serve people, and the degree to which we don't serve people—that's our job to figure those things out.

In reflecting on his own values and how they are linked to the values of Ben & Jerry's, Matthew talks about his understanding of commerce as a means of creating a more inclusive, equitable society: "I am unequivocally a believer in the power of commerce, the power of competition, the power of people trying to make the world better for humans." As we discussed this, Matthew made the distinction between commerce and capitalism, focusing on the importance of the former as a mode of exchange. "You know how to thatch a roof? I have cows. Let's exchange. That's commerce. And

---

* A concept where, if the company prospers, then all the stakeholders connected to the business prosper, too.

so, I believe that commerce can make the world better. Unequivocally. We have benefited from it. I mean, I can drink the water out of my tap and not die . . . Yet, as Greta Thunberg says, the answer is not endless growth," says Matthew. "The world doesn't need 25,000 ice cream companies. It maybe needs a smaller number of them doing a better job with dairy and cocoa and whatnot. But the point I'm making is *that* is my vision for business and commerce, and I never really understood that until recent years." Tying together his values of fairness, hard work, equity, and inclusion, Matthew talked about how much of capitalism, as distinct from commerce, has for centuries been about the "marginalization of people, which is linked to exclusion, the lack of inclusivity. And your business can grow significantly more when you include more people." An important question for Matthew that all business leaders could ask themselves is, "How are you lowering the bar on boundaries to inclusion in your business?"

Famous for its social activism, Ben & Jerry's has supported campaigns around marriage equality, fair trade, climate change, Occupy Wall Street, and Black Lives Matter, to name but a few. And when I asked Matthew about how these values of social activism coexist within a competitive business environment, he made some interesting distinctions between zero-sum and win-win scenarios, competition and winning:

> For me, it's performance versus winning; some days you win, some days you don't, but every day you can work hard. First of all, at a broad level, I believe that things that are zero-sum are usually bad. Now, it depends . . . let me use a couple of different examples. One of them is "we win, the environment loses." So that zero-sum game is broken, it's destroying the Earth, and we're either going to fix it or we're going to go extinct. Our natural resources, our natural world continues to deteriorate—that type of a zero-sum is actually

a path to death. Now, let me take a very different example of zero-sum: Ben and Jerry's versus one of our archrivals in ice cream.

I intend to kick their ass, and I want to beat them decisively in the market.

Now, at the end of the day, if we're successful, their business may suffer and decline. You could say, "Well, that's a zero-sum game." I say no, it isn't a zero-sum game; if we are giving people a better product, better value proposition, one that actually fits with peoples' values in the world, we will have actually made the world better. Now you could say that's crazy because you would have put a lot of people out of a job. Yeah, but if they were working for a business that doesn't deserve the right to operate because consumers are not choosing that product, that's not a zero-sum game. There are times when people get put out of a job, but it's usually because senior managers fuck things up. There are thousands of people depending on my team and I to not fuck it up, and if they all lose their job because our competitor beats us, maybe we deserve to be beaten.

As we finished our conversation, we focused on the importance of a leader being aware of their personal values and how these values can be enacted within their leadership context. It led to some fascinating insights on how Matthew, who runs a billion-dollar business, has evolved over time in his understanding of achieving results, and how this in turn has impacted his attitude and approach to the people who work with him.

Constant improvement and results are big values for me . . . Earlier in my career, I'd say I struggled in my relationship with results because I was afraid about whether or not I could deliver them . . . but I like to win, I'm a competitive guy, and I want to know what you did to make something better, and if we don't reach our goals, that's not the end of the world. That's not failure. Failure is not making the effort to make something better . . . I very much value people working to make things better . . . Everybody is rowing, you don't have to be rowing as hard as everybody else. There may be times you need to take a break, maybe you've just got one hand on the oar, but if you're sitting there and you're letting everybody else row—going back to fairness, a lot of these things overlap—for me, performance and results are linked to fairness. We don't come here to sit around and collect paychecks. We came here to do something and to do something together. All organizations are about people coming together because of some overlap and desire about what they want to do or achieve or accomplish or change in the world. And therefore, it is incumbent on you, by showing up, that you are going to row. If not, move to a different place in the boat or get out of the boat to some other boat.

In preparation for our conversation, Matthew completed the reflective exercise at the end of this chapter. This served as an aid in clarifying the values that have been most foundational to who he is and the leader he has become. But before it's our turn to engage with this exercise, let's first explore a psychological model that provides a wider context for *why* a conscious awareness of our values is important in the first place.

LOGICAL LEVELS MODEL

Building on elements from the work of Cambridge mathematician Bertrand Russell, the English anthropologist Gregory Bateson wrote a book called *Steps to an Ecology of Mind* (1972). Bateson's work developed some aspects of Russell's understanding of logic, applying it to the interrelationships of different systems that affect the human psyche. Bateson subsequently came up with four "criteria of mind," which theorized how mental processes develop.[2] In a similar approach to how Russell viewed some aspects of logic within mathematics, Bateson stated, "A mind is an aggregate of interacting parts or components" that interact and transform each other in "a hierarchy of logical types."[3] Bateson's work was further developed by one of his students, Robert Dilts, into a model of personal change that was first known as "Neurological Levels" and has come to be referred to as "Logical Levels."[4]

As one of the founders of NLP (neuro-linguistic programming), Dilts was interested in models of personal development that focused on the relationship between our thinking, our communication (especially the language we use), and our patterns of behavior.

In 1990, Dilts published *Changing Belief Systems with NLP* and subsequently, because of his development of Bateson's work, produced a model called "Levels of Experience"[5] that described six "Logical Levels" as part of a "Co-Alignment Process."[6] Like any model, it's useful to a point and has its own limitations (critics of NLP claim it is pseudoscientific, while its proponents tend not to be solely reliant on the scientific method as an epistemology). But it can help us gain some understanding into the underlying factors that influence how we behave within our environment and provides us with some insights as to how inner change takes place. In the diagram on page 107, let's examine the Logical Levels model from top to bottom, starting with our environment and moving to behaviors, capabilities, values, identities, and meaning.[7]

Changes to the composition of one level can impact the levels above and below. To bring about change within this interconnected system, we need to find the variables within each level, the aspects of our Inner World that are open to change as we mature

Logical Levels and True and False Self

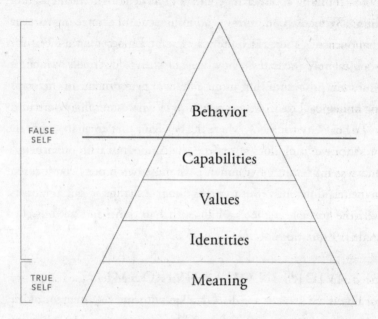

Environment

FALSE SELF

Behavior

Capabilities

Values

Identities

TRUE SELF

Meaning

as leaders—from the capabilities (skills and experience) we have to the values and identities that we embody. Introducing a different capability, value, or identity will have a knock-on effect throughout the system. And it's just a matter of trial and error, of changing these variables across the different levels to see the impact that this has on the system as a whole.

Another way of thinking about this is that we find out where there is misalignment in a system and then seek to influence that system in any place to bring about greater alignment and congruence. And the "system," in this case, is the interplay of the various elements within our Inner World that affect our leadership in the environment of our Outer World.

EXTERNAL AND INTERNAL CHANGES TO OUR ENVIRONMENT

When thinking about change, much of leadership literature has traditionally focused on how we can influence and change our external environment. There's definitely a time and place for this. But this book is more focused on how we can change internally, which, in time, will profoundly affect our external environment. In this framing of Logical Levels, we pay attention to what is misaligned between us and our environment, where the behavior that emanates from the presence we bring does not effectively connect us with other people and systems in our environment. We must tweak our behaviors and do things differently. But to bring about a change in our behaviors, we need to look at the capabilities that we have and ask ourselves some key questions.

BEHAVIORS IN OUR ENVIRONMENT

Ideally, the behaviors we display align with the requirement of our leadership environment. For example, for Matthew McCarthy, his communication, actions, and decisions needed to be aligned with the commercial realities of the business in a way that was inclusive of all stakeholders and aligned with the Ben & Jerry's values of being environmentally and financially sustainable. Consistently aligning our behaviors to our environment is very challenging. Everyone else we lead is part of our environment, and they experience our behaviors all the time, often in ways that we cannot even see ourselves. These two sets of environment and behaviors, at the top of the diagram, are visible for all to see.

CAPABILITIES

Do we have the skills and experience required that will enable us to behave differently? Aside from interpersonal skills and capabilities, such as self-awareness and emotional intelligence, do we have the requisite talents, or have we received the appropriate training for what we're trying to do? For example, in the life of a corporate leader, are we known for our great budgeting, vision casting, planning, or marketing? For our communication, for our social media influencing? When it comes to professions, we either have or haven't trained in a particular aspect of the law, in a certain medical procedure, or in a specific coding language that our environment requires. And in the absence of these training courses, we simply do not have the capability to behave any differently.

Or maybe we do have a basic level of some of these capabilities and skills, but we find it difficult to dig deeper into them in a way that affects our behavior. If this is the case, we need to go further down the Logical Levels model to find out where the bottleneck is, what else is impacting our capabilities that in turn is preventing us from behaving in the ways most required in our environment. We need to understand the best fit between what our environment needs and the capability we have to influence people and systems in our environment from a place of deep presence (we'll explore this in detail in chapter ten). To lead effectively, it goes without saying that we'll need to have certain technical skills and abilities (e.g., leading the IT in an organization will require a fundamental understanding of IT systems—otherwise, we won't be respected by those we are trying to lead).

VALUES

The next level down is our values. What do we value? What do we care about? What's important to us? Some of our values are very consciously held—we're very aware of them, and we can name them right now. For most people that I work with, honesty or integrity usually features in their top ten list of values. For business owners, adventure often features as a value. For more traditional professionals, stability or safety is frequently mentioned.

But we have other, unconsciously held values, which most of us only become aware of once they're challenged. For example, we're happy at work and doing very well in our role, and then somebody comes into the organization at a higher level than us and tells us to stop performing tasks that we have been doing for a long time. Or they say they're going to rationalize our role, so we need to find something different. And this triggers something in us. We move into our sympathetic nervous system state. It's not that we mind being told what to do. But as we reflect on this experience, we realize that autonomy and freedom are key values for us, and we were triggered because we weren't included in any way in the decision-making process.

A key way of understanding what our values are is noticing where we invest our energy and what we do with our time. We'll complete an exercise around this at the end of the chapter, but let's first examine what else influences the formation of our values from within the Logical Levels model.

IDENTITIES

What have been the most impactful pursuits, life experiences, and activities that have influenced how we think about and view ourselves? We were all children at some point, and that may or may not have been a deeply influential identity for us. But everyone has a unique set of identities that they feel defines them. I know of doctors who will tell anyone they meet about their profession, so strong is their sense of identity with their role; and I know of other doctors who are nonplussed about their job and hardly talk about it. Some people strongly identify as being a good friend, an athlete, as someone who's funny, an extrovert, or a socialite. Others identify as being a reflector, a writer, an academic, a coach, a parent, a caregiver. We can have unique monikers for our identities—such as Adventurer, Comedian, or Leader, which we'll explore in the next chapter—but fundamentally, we need to have some alignment between our identities. Otherwise, we will be split, living one life at home and one life at work, showing up in different ways with different people. This chameleon-like way of interacting with various individuals and groups is a common experience for most throughout childhood, adolescence, and early adulthood. During these times, we're learning about who we are, trying to explore the different facets of our personality and experimenting with what we want to be known for by others. But as leaders, whose very presence influences others, it's crucial that there's a more coherent alignment across all our identities, a red thread that links them together in their relational dance. For example, Leader of Excellence and Caring Mother, identities that may seem to be at odds to others, both value hard work and compassion for other people. So, one might ensure that these two powerful identities are in regular dialogue regarding how to share their time and energy at home and at work.

If our identities aren't being inwardly felt or outwardly expressed in ways that we value, ways that feel balanced and authentic, then we'll struggle to fully access our capabilities and, in turn, to behave in the most resourceful ways in our environment. We need to become aware of our identities so that we can express them. And then we can more fully understand the sense of meaning and purpose that they allow us to embody and enact in our lives.

MEANING

Originally, the word "spirituality" was used instead for this level of the model. But, bringing this model into corporate environments, many consultants swapped the word "spirituality" for "purpose." The concept of having a purpose, or uncovering one's purpose, has been a buzzword in the corporate world for at least ten years. It can mean anything from why an organization exists to what motivates individuals to lead and everything in between. However, I prefer to use the word "meaning" instead of "purpose" or "spirituality," as I find it straddles the deeply spiritual connotation of *being* with the crucially important emphasis on *doing*, or acting with conviction, that comes from having a clarity of purpose.

Without meaning, our energies will wane more quickly, and we'll give up more easily when challenges arise. We'll find ways to unconsciously self-sabotage and adversely impact the relationships and environments that we influence. Having meaning helps us focus on the essence of who we are, why we exist, and therefore how we lead and influence. As we move from the identities we've inhabited in our deepest sense of meaning, purpose, or spirituality, we're really moving from our False Self—who we've been socialized to become in order to find our place in society—into our True Self. More on this in chapter six.

CONTEMPLATIVE LEADERSHIP AND VALUES

As we've been exploring thus far in this book, our ability to lead in a contemplative manner emanates from our capacity to be deeply present to ourselves and, in turn, to be present to and connected with others. Exploring or reassessing our consciously and unconsciously held values is a helpful starting point to understanding the presence we embody in each moment. It uncovers what motivates us, what we most care about, and how these values in turn impact our everyday leadership behaviors. Essentially, they give us an insight into how others experience us. And if we want to make any personal changes to our lived presence and connection with others, then this layer of the Logical Levels model is a great place to start. Over the next two chapters, we'll build on these values, linking them to our identities and our sense of meaning and purpose.

REFLECTIVE EXERCISE

As we shine a light on our own inner workings, we can become less attached to the unconscious narratives and scripts that guide our every leadership instinct.

1. Personal Life
   From the following list, choose the four to five values that best describe what you value as most important in your personal life.

MY VALUES

Achievement	Advancement	Adventure	Arts	Authority
Autonomy	Challenge	Change	Community	Competition
Cooperation	Creativity	Decisiveness	Democracy	Environmental responsibility
Effectiveness	Family	Fast-pace	Financial gain	Free time
Friendships	Harmony	Health	Helping others	Honesty
Independence	Influencing others	Integrity	Intellect	Knowledge
Leadership	Location	Love	Loyalty	Meaningful work
Money	Pleasure	Power	Pressure	Privacy
Promotion	Public service	Quality work	Recognition	Relationships
Reputation	Security	Self-respect	Serenity	Sophistication
Spirituality	Stability	Status	Trust	Truth
Variety	Volunteering	Wealth	Wisdom	Other: _____

2. Career
   Now write down the four to five values that best describe what you most value in your career. (These may be related to your previous answers or could be totally different.) Don't edit yourself; go with your gut instinct.

3. Your Organization
   Next, write down the four to five values that best describe your experience of what is most valued within your organization.

These words will describe the overarching cultural values of your organization. (If helpful, you can make the distinction between the cultural values of your whole organization and the cultural values that exist within your team.)

4. Your Leadership
   Finally, write down the four to five values that underpin the values you espouse as a leader.

5. From your answers above, which values are similar across all four categories: Personal Life, Career, Your Organization, and Your Leadership?

←――――――――――――――――――――――――――――――――→

1   10
Hardly living   Embodying this
this value   value each day

6. Focusing on the values that overlap across several of the categories, rank each of them on a scale of 1 to 10, where 1 means that you're hardly living out this value at all and 10 means that you're embodying this value daily.

7. Reflecting on the Logical Levels model, whereby a changed emphasis in your values can lead to a knock-on effect in your capabilities, behavior, and beyond, which values would you like to embody more fully?

8. What simple, practical actions can you commit to that will help you focus on these values (e.g., meditating once a day to experience more serenity or speaking your mind in meetings to embody honesty)?

9. What does this exercise tell you about who you are, your deepest sense of identity?

Chapter 6

IDENTITIES AND PERSONAS

Tear off the mask. Your face is glorious.
—Jalal ad-Din Rumi

Margaret Wheatley is a leadership consultant, speaker, and best-selling author who, for decades, has worked with myriad corporations, governments, not-for-profits, and community-based organizations. In 1992, she shot to fame with the publication of her first book, *Leadership and the New Science*. In it, she challenged contemporary understandings of business and leadership that relied on the hierarchical, predictable, cause-and-effect approach of a Newtonian understanding of the world. Instead, Margaret (who goes by Meg) examined the implications of chaos theory and quantum physics on how we look at the world, how "order is natural" but not something that we can control, how relationships "are the basic organizing unit of life," and how participation and cooperation with others are crucial for how we navigate our interconnected world.[1] Considering this was before the internet was used for business and before social media existed, her approach was both challenging of the status quo and prescient of technological developments to come.

"A big part of my role in life was to introduce people within the field of leadership and management and organization . . . to the possibility that there's a whole other way of leading people," Meg says. "I thought it was so self-evident that it would absolutely be accepted . . . my publisher, when he read the manuscript, said, 'This book will make you famous,' and it did."

Reflecting on the source of her energy and focus, Meg recalls some of the important people and experiences in her life that have influenced the roles she's had and the person she's become: "My grandmother, Irma Lindheim, was one of the outstanding women in the creation of the state of Israel. She was a dominant force in my life and where I got all my definition of what a meaningful life is: it's a life of service and dedication and writing. When I was six years old, she said, 'Meggie, you need to be a writer.'. . . my English father gave me a deep understanding of nature and of life, of the Celtic Druid ways. The land in England is still magical; that's where I got my mystic self from. That focus on the mystic, animated Earth."

Meg spent two and a half years in the Peace Corps, teaching English in what was then a very traditional culture in South Korea. Although initially drawn to Buddhism there, she realized that "Buddhism would require a lot of discipline" and that she "wasn't going to go on that path when I was just a ripening young woman filled with the desire for life." From Korea, she moved home and directed community-based educational efforts in poor communities outside of New York City. But she sensed that there was more for her to do and decided to study for her master's degree. Under the tutelage of Neil Postman, she researched how the introduction of new technology to political campaigns (television then, in the 1960s) had created changes to voter behaviors, expectations, and culture. And from there she went to Harvard for her doctorate and worked closely with the famous consultant Rosabeth Moss Kanter. All of these formational experiences and relationships led to Meg founding the Berkana Institute and, more recently, Warriors for the Human Spirit Training, first consulting with corporations but then switching to more community-based, federal, educational, and healthcare organizations from the late 1990s onward. "As I aged in that work," she says, "I became more generous, more patient, and really understood the depth of challenging someone's worldview. I think it's essential work. It's definitely my work . . . but I understand that you're asking someone to take away the foundations of their work or the way they have constructed their life and their world."

From her initial assumption that people will change when presented with evidence-based facts, Meg realized that there was so much else at play in influencing how open we are to considering a change in our perspectives: "I do now understand what it takes to shift the way we see the world. When you really get into the heart of everything, our image [of ourselves] is something that we have interpreted and made sense of unconsciously and created this self that doesn't exist." For Meg, deconstructing and working with "this self that doesn't exist" became central to her work "with leaders and activists, as Warriors for the Human Spirit, as champions for people and the spirit of life of the planet." Far from a mere theoretical approach, Meg has firsthand experience of facing this "self that doesn't exist." Her initial response when she became famous for writing *Leadership and the New Science* was that she was "afraid of losing [her] soul."

In 2010, she began doing long retreats (sixty to one hundred days) every winter as a student of American Buddhist nun Pema Chödrön. During a sixty-day retreat in 2014, she had an experience of existential fear, a sense that she was a complete failure. The previous summer, she'd "had this incredible experience" of sharing the stage "with the Dalai Lama, and then I'd received these rare and profound initiations from [Pema Chödrön's] Tibetan Buddhist teacher—but then when I got into retreat, I just went down, down, down, down. And each time I felt, 'I've hit bottom,' but then there would be another bottom to hit. And I finally did hit bottom, and my last act was to call Pema and say, 'I need to tell you, I am a total failure.' And her instantaneous response was, 'Oh, I wonder how old that is?' She came and worked with me and gave me practices that helped lift me out. It was this practice, which I still use quite a lot, of *Tonglen*." Literally meaning "sending and receiving," Tonglen is a practice of using one's own suffering to connect with and relieve the suffering of others.[2]

As she continued this practice, her "fear, sense of failure, and rage" began to dissipate—and with them Meg's constructed identities that had defined themselves by "failure or success," by getting their way or not, by controlling their environment to achieve their desired outcomes. Meg experienced a reordering of her identities, a fresh perspective of who she really was and what was important for her to do.

Meg had already connected deeply with the work of Chögyam Trungpa, the Tibetan Buddhist monk who founded Shambhala Training (which brings together people of all faiths through teachings and meditative practices of awareness and nonaggression in the pursuit of an enlightened society).[3] She'd been using the prophecy of the return of the Shambhala warriors since the mid-nineties. As a result of her years of deep retreat training in Trungpa's teachings and practices, she shifted the focus of her work with leaders to create Warrior Training. A warrior, according to Meg, is someone who trains themselves "with the weapons of compassion and insight" to be used in service to their time. "History shows that, in difficult times, only a few people rise to counteract and contradict the depravity and despair that's going on," she explains. "To be an effective warrior, exercising the skills of insight and compassion, requires rigorous training, training of your mind, training of your perceptual abilities, training in mind–body awareness." Meg defines a warrior as "a sane human being willing to serve in an inhumane, insane time."

"When I look back at my life," says Meg, "I realize that I have had incredible gifts. Very different qualities. I have never felt impeded. I really just felt that if I choose to do it, it's going to happen. And I've always had a strong sense of intuition that has helped, and then I had been gifted with the most incredible teachers who were all for supporting me to do my work and helped me define what my work is." In the new edition of her book *Who Do We Choose To Be?* Meg quotes from the yogi Sadhguru, who very clearly states, "If you do not do what you cannot do, that is not a problem. But if you do not do what is yours to do, you are a disaster, a wasted life."[4] It's "stark," says Meg, "but it's very real. I mean, just keep on doing what's yours to do and try to wean yourself off outcomes and expectations, because who knows where it's going to go? Who are we to complain or to get in the way, or to doubt or to falter? Just stay in the middle of the river, as the Hopi prophecy tells us."

OUR IDENTITIES

As Meg alludes to, when we look back on our lives, we can see that there was a season for different activities, a time when we were drawn to exploring one part of ourselves and expressing it in certain ways. And as Meg sensed as a young woman during her first experiences of Buddhism in Korea, there's also a time for us to pay attention to our intuition yet wait until we feel ready to explore this longing, this part of ourselves. As our values become clear and as our narratives develop over the course of many years, we can experience an evolution in our worldview. Part of this shift takes place when our self-image, the identities we have "unconsciously created of this self that doesn't exist," evolve and develop. These identities, these ways of perceiving who we are in the world, are influenced by many factors, including key relationships and role models in our lives (e.g., Meg's grandmother and father were significant for her), the cultures and countries we come from, and our life experiences, from college life to service work. Growing up, we are drawn to certain role models, lifestyles, and ways of working and living in the world. We cultivate different identities and perform specific roles, such as daughter, sibling, parent, leader, teacher, or friend. These identities help us live our lives in effective ways, as they provide us with the boundaries we need to focus our energies on specific tasks, roles, and contexts.

So far, we've been exploring the various perspectives and narratives that we have around our leadership. We have begun to look at how some of these narratives have come from other people and how others emanate from deep within ourselves. Many of these narratives have served us and continue to serve us, but other narratives can limit us from being our very best selves and leading and influencing to our full potential. And regardless of the source of these narratives, they all affect our nervous system states, which impacts our presence, how we are emotionally connected to ourselves and others, and, in turn, how we show up to lead and influence in each moment. But as we look at the interplay of the different aspects of our physiology, our emotions, our thinking, and our values, we need to go one level deeper and understand the various identities we have that influence how we view ourselves. Just like Meg, it is crucial that we are open to having our deep-seated understanding of ourselves evolve and change over time. This gives space for us to deconstruct and explore "this self that doesn't exist." It's transitioning from the False Self of who we think we are toward the True Self of who we really are. We just need to get out of our own way for long enough to see it and then to start to inhabit it. There is no simple, clear-cut approach for how to move from our False Self to our True Self; we never finally get there. But it's the process of exploring, of seeking to understand and know ourselves, that counts. That's how we more fully inhabit our Whole Self, how we develop our presence so that we can better connect with and lead others. We need to take time to reflect and understand what have been the most impactful life experiences, relationships, and activities that have influenced how we think about ourselves. What this involves is, essentially, an exploration of the many facets of our ego.

EGO

In contemporary parlance, the word "ego" is often used as a pejorative term. "She's got a big ego" or "His ego is getting in the way" are not very flattering statements. But an ego, in and of itself, isn't necessarily something bad. It can be something healthy and helpful. In fact, in the sense that I'm using the word, "ego" is a neutral term that can have very positive facets as well as very negative ones. It all depends on one's perspective and awareness of one's ego.

The following pages draw on the subpersonalities work of the transpersonal and integrative psychotherapist John Rowan, as well as the language and structure of the ego with its composite personas from the analytical psychologist Carl Jung. We'll focus on the practical ways we can map out our internal world by first getting to know the various personas, also known as identities, that we have, which directly influence how we lead and how others experience our leadership presence.

Attaching to certain identities that allow us to socially fit in with our environment is a crucial part of development when we are young. Jung talked about the importance of building the container of our identity through the attachments that we form with individuals and groups during the "morning of life," the first forty years or so that bring us up to about midway through our lifespan.[5] Jung called these different parts of our identity our "personas"—literally from the Latin, "per sonare," to sound through, a persona was an acoustical resonance mask that Etruscan, Greek, and Roman actors wore. The shape of the mask helped project their voices while playing a particular role. It's important for our healthy development that we try out various identities as we grow up and begin to learn about our own ability to influence and lead others. But there comes a time when we need to remove these masks and to stop attaching to the same old roles we've always played.

To integrate the learnings of all these roles, we need to no longer be attached to any one of them. This is scary and risky, as it can feel like we're losing touch with who we are, with what we've been known for over a prolonged period. For example, there can be an identity crisis for parents who, after giving decades of their lives to raising their children, watch the last of their offspring leave home. Who *are* they if they're not dedicating much of their time and energy to the daily practicalities of parenting? Similarly, for the leader who, after years, switches organizations, changes industries, or takes early retirement, so much of what they've been known for—their skills, public image, title—has been enmeshed in their role as a long-term leader at one particular organization. Moving away can feel strange, confusing, discombobulating.

But the alternative, where we remain attached to our old identities, is one where we must take on more and more control in an ever-evolving, complex environment. We hold on tightly to make sure things don't change within us, which prevents us from allowing others to change as well. We insist that our teams continue performing in the same ways as before, that our leadership strategies and their implementation remain the same; all of our leadership initiatives continue to come from the same playbook we've always used, and any external change (e.g., team members leaving or significant shifts in our field or industry or in market trends) are threats that we must clamp down on and control in any way we can.

Each of these identities has their own backstory, and we'll seek to understand where they've come from, who they are today, and, crucially, what they want and need. As we explore the relationships that these identities have with each other, what they each offer and need, we'll get to understand more of what drives our leadership at its very core.

This helps to shine a light on where we experience ongoing tensions in how we lead and why we are not always able to do the things that we want to do or that we say we'll do. It enables us to uncover competing motivations within and explore the internal dialogues necessary to move beyond contradictory actions and blockages—where we *want* to do something, but, for some reason, we're just not able to follow through. Essentially, as we explore the various identities of our ego, we may discover different internal narratives that have competing goals with whatever it is that we consciously think we want.

IDENTITIES EXERCISE

The following exercise helps us map out our identities and their evolving relationships with each other. The best way to understand this exercise is to see a worked-through example. Out of the many identities that resonate with me, I'm going to show you a sample of three of them, exploring who they are and then bringing them into conversation with each other.

To help us distinguish one from the other, it's helpful to name our identities with monikers based on a dominant characteristic that summarizes who they are. For this example, my three identities are named Efficient, Adventurous, and Father/King. I begin by outlining each one's composition under the same headings that you'll use when you complete the exercise:

1. Characteristics
2. Desires
3. Age
4. Emotions
5. Senses
6. Triggers
7. Shadow:
   a. What are they not aware of that the other identities seem to know about them?
   b. What aspects of themselves do they shy away from, deny, or doubt?
8. Connections to others
   a. How do they view and feel about the other identities?
   b. What, if anything, do they want from the other identities?
   c. How do they want to interact with the other identities?

EXAMPLES OF THREE OF PATRICK'S IDENTITIES

EFFICIENT
1. Characteristics: Corporate, slick, clear, calm, prepared.
2. Desires: To do a really good job at everything. To make life as seamless as possible so that I can enjoy the more important aspects of life, such as relationships, quality time with loved ones, adventures, creativity, and rest.
3. Age: 23 (the age I was for my first management consulting role). Also feels 46 at times, mature and calm—typically the prime of a consultant's life.
4. Emotions: Mature and calm.
5. Senses:

a. Sees possibilities.

b. Hears appreciation.

c. Touches complex perspectives, rooms, companies, and situations with confidence.

d. Tastes a slightly dry mouth due to so many activities; drinks water and coffee in the morning; also tastes the frustration of inefficiencies, intransigence, the active blocking of worthwhile projects.

e. Smells food in the oven that's ready to eat as soon as we dock the boat at the marina. It's a well-timed arrival that's coordinated with food planning on board—very efficient.

6. Triggers: Unnecessarily inefficient people and systems

7. Shadow:

a. What are they not aware of that the other identities seem to know about them? He can seem "cut and dry" to others, as well as impatient.

b. What aspects of themselves do they shy away from, deny, or doubt? He is often scared of his potential and denies the possibilities of his capabilities.

8. Connections to others: (I'm not completing this part of the exercise yet, but I'll build it up as new identities are revealed.)

a. How do they view and feel about the other identities?

b. What, if anything, do they want from the other identities?

c. How do they want to interact with the other identities?

ADVENTUROUS

1. Characteristics: Excited by life; loves fun, trips, journeys, challenges, and shared experiences with others, like hiking, sailing, camping, being outdoors—always thinking of what's possible and what's exciting.

2. Desires: Moments and journeys of wonder, appreciation of life's beauty, shared experiences, small challenges, seizing the

day, and connecting with others with fun chats and deep conversations.

3. Age: 34—a time when I had more adventures and was fitter.

4. Emotions: Composed, excited, prepared, flexible, open, spontaneous.

5. Senses:

   a. Sees flash torches and head torches and twinkling stars in Glendalough's sky (a favorite hiking valley of mine).

   b. Hears waves of wind in the treetops, the hum of a boat's diesel engine, winches loaded with ropes spinning on a boat, focused chatter among the crew, zips of tents and sleeping bags being closed, and heavy breathing into my neck warmer in the cold morning light of an uphill hike.

   c. Touches snow, pine trees, a hot mug of tea, and the helm of the boat.

   d. Tastes protein bars, ice-cold mountain water, and stale tea bags at the bottom of my thermos flask.

   e. Smells bacon sandwiches at dawn on the boat and pinecones in the forest.

6. Trigger: Poor planning regarding the weather, a trail that overly challenges people or leads to a waste of time and energy, "roughing it" unnecessarily (linked to my Efficient identity).

7. Shadow:

   a. What are they not aware of that the other identities seem to know about them? He is sometimes too careful and safe.

   b. What aspects of themselves do they shy away from, deny, or doubt? He's not vocal enough when unhappy with the poor planning of others.

8. Connections to others:

   a. How do they view and feel about the other identities? Loves the Efficient identity—really respects him when it comes to planning. Efficient has the right idea—do things simply and well, and then you'll have a lot of time to have fun and connect with others.

b. What, if anything, do they want from the other identities? To continue to learn from Efficient but also to have the freedom to be more spontaneous, to trust themselves that playing it safe so much of the time reduces spontaneity. Since becoming a dad, "efficient" and "safe" have come to characterize so much of the way Adventurous interacts with others.

c. How do they want to interact with the other identities? He needs to lean in to Efficient a bit more, as Adventurous has become too focused on "getting things right." So many of the opportunities for Adventurous have recently become very sanitized. It's time to trust himself more and lean in to Efficient. I feel that Adventurous is "less than" Efficient; Efficient is older (46 for sure) and more responsible, while Adventurous is only 34 and not quite as focused on maximizing his time and energy. Adventurous and Efficient need to go on a hike together, a hike that Adventurous runs, and have a talk on the trail about how they're going to develop their relationship moving forward. In fact, this would be a relief to Efficient, as he's already shouldering too much responsibility as it is. Efficient is very much the dominant identity in this relationship, and he really wants to see Adventurous step up and express himself more.

FATHER/KING

N.B. This is a very metaphorical description of my "Father/King" identity, using archetypal language and imagery from a fairytale. I was relaxing into this identities exercise and was free-associating in my writing—I hadn't expected these words to emerge. But I share them as an example of a different style of writing that may be beneficial when completing this exercise.

1. Characteristics: Present, all-encompassing, arms wide open, aware of his realm of influence and the boundaries around it. Caring and kind. Insightful and wise; has learned over the years to trust his intuition. Protects and defends, keeps a sense of order and safety for those within his realm. Has learned to have stronger defenses and boundaries with challenging people and situations, which sometimes means proactively targeting threats.

2. Desires: To be present and connected to self and others; to be in the here and now while also being open to and aware of the larger story, the bigger picture of the evolution of the cosmos, and his tiny role within that. Also desires, however, to be totally present to his role within that, providing support and care, space for creativity and intuition, protection, and strength to himself and to others who come within his realm. So far, he's not ever sought to expand his realm; he's focused more on inhabiting what is already there, and, in time, he might be open to expansion—but he doesn't *need* his realm to expand.

3. Age: 0 to 10,000; at times he has the innocence and wonder of a newborn baby in their moments of quiet and intimacy with their evolving new life, and at other times he takes the longer view of 10,000 years, of the rise and fall of civilizations and habitats, of the cyclical nature of evolution and change. He modulates between these ages, dipping into whatever age seems to best suit the current situation he is facing.

4. Emotions: Centered. Expressive and adaptable. Embraces the music of dirges and the emotion of sadness; the exhilaration and excitement of drums at a tournament or their solemnity before a battle or a sacred rite; the poignant and lyrical music of expression and love.

5. Senses:

   a. Sees a tent within which he rules and is a judge for justice. People coming to him for advice and insight. A campfire surrounded by a circle of stones the size of seats, where elders and visitors gather for discussions at night. Warriors on duty, protecting the tent, the camp, the village, and the borders of the entire realm. Poets, musicians, doctors, healers, working in various parts of the village, expressing themselves and caring for others. Magicians and monks who live on the edge of the camp—they come with insights and heightened senses of awareness on myriad topics and then retreat to be alone with nature and the Great Spirit. Sees his son, a young man now, proudly walking over to him to speak about a topic they'll both enjoy discussing.

   b. Hears the busyness of some parts of the camp, the silence of the tent when he is making a decision, the quiet breeze in between the statements of the magicians and monks who come to share their insights, the stomp and march of warriors, and the jangle of their armor as they come on duty and inspect the documents and wares of visitors and those returning home.

   c. Touches the rounded mahogany of the simple throne beneath his right hand, feels the soft yellow robes along his forearms as he moves during the sitting of his council.

   d. Tastes the clean, cool water from his cup, which keeps him alert during the quiet court sessions in which he presides; later, tastes the delicious Bordeaux wine that has just been served to him at the perfect temperature.

   e. Smells the fresh air, the straw, the burning incense in the anteroom, the smoldering beginnings of the campfire that has just been lit for the evening of storytelling and feasting outside.

6. Triggers: Aides who fuss, visitors who mislead and lie, verbose courtiers who attempt to curry favor.

7. Shadow:

   a. What are they not aware of that the other identities seem to know about them? Can be too passive; he's often not out on the borders defending the realm. Also, he is too focused on the defense of what he has rather than on expanding his benign realm to influence others for good who want to participate in his realm. Certainly has a superior air; he's not that showy or flashy, but he can be a little self-satisfied. He distances himself from other Fathers, other Kings, because it would be so much hassle to have to negotiate with them and engage in bargaining and making agreements.

   b. What aspects of themselves do they shy away from, deny, or doubt? He lives in his own version of paradise. He knows it's not perfect, and he's always working on developing it for its inhabitants and for the good of those friendly neighbors nearby. But his vision can be too limited; he is being invited into a cosmic realm far beyond his vision for integration and his 10,000-year perspective— try a 4.6-billion-year perspective. He needs to be willing to let go of what he's got to make room for what he's being invited into next.

8. Connections to others:

   a. How do they view and feel about the other identities? He loves them dearly. Adventurous is close to his heart; he yearns to be out there much more with him. He sees that he's toned things down a bit recently—the wisdom of the magicians and monks has manifested itself in the form of

Efficient, who has taken the lead in guiding Adventurous. Efficient is actually controlling Adventurous, and Father/King is going to take Efficient aside this evening at the campfire, fill him with a few glasses of good wine, and have a heart-to-heart with him about how he's taking over and setting too much of the tone around the realm of late.

As for how the other identities feel about Father/King, they respect him deeply. Adventurous wishes that Father/King were more adventurous; they've had days when Father/King and him were one. Father/King taught Adventurous how to be himself, encouraged him to take risks, showed him how to run with the animals and survive with almost nothing in the wilderness before always returning home to invigorate others with his gifts and tales of adventure. Father/King gave him permission, and Adventurous wants to see Father/King come out of his tent and go on more hunts and adventures with him. Efficient really respects Father/King. He's glad he's taken his judicial wisdom and educational roles so much more seriously over the last few years. He's going to get a shock when Father/King asks him to sit back a little, to tone things down and create more room for Adventurous and the other identities.

b. What, if anything, do they want from the other identities? For Efficient to sit back a little, to take the pressure off, and for Adventurous to stand up, speak up, and go adventuring much more, without any plan or any need for permission from the Father/King.

c. How do they want to interact with the other identities? Have a drink and a chat with Efficient and ask him to relax a little. If that doesn't work, Father/King will employ his tougher-edged warrior side (honed over years of being on active duty as a young man) and make it very clear that

Efficient is in a bottleneck of growth and will have to take two steps back now in order to take three steps forward in the future. With Adventurous, he wants to tell him, "Go out and run free. Take a night away; go with the hunt. Stop to sleep or else track and hunt all night long—whatever you want! Get back into the old patterns of being alive. You're less yourself than you've been before. We need you to be *you*. We all need to be inspired, to be reminded of what it's like to run free and adventure. And after your first night away, I'll come with you on your second adventure in the coming two weeks. So be ready. I'll arrive at your door at dusk, all packed and ready to follow your lead into the night."

As you can see, this was a creative and spontaneous exercise for me. As you engage in your own exercise, try to be open to it going in any number of directions. I started out in a logical frame of mind, beginning with my very pragmatic Efficient identity. I was sitting in a little cabin within a valley in Ireland, surrounded on three sides by trees, and one side gave me a beautiful view down the valley. I wrote by hand in my journal, and as I looked out the window, listening to the wind in the trees, my thinking slowed, and I gradually moved into a more creative state (my ventral vagal nervous system state). It took over an hour to move from Efficient into Adventurous and Father/King, but you can clearly see the shift in my thinking from literal to imaginative as the exercise progressed.

Taking your time with this exercise and finding a conducive environment in which to complete it can make a significant difference to your experience. If you don't feel like you're ready, or you just don't want to do it, I'd encourage you to skip this exercise and return to it when the time feels right. If this strikes you as "just another task," then please move on for now.

REFLECTIVE EXERCISE

MY IDENTITIES

STEP 1: LIST THEM

What are all the identities that you adopt, or have regularly adopted, from time to time? What are they called? Let their names be a descriptor for yourself as to who they are. For example, here are mine:

- Efficient
- Adventurous
- Father/King
- Creative Daydreamer
- Activist Healer
- Spiritually Centered

STEP 2: TRINKET

I suggest that you find a paperweight or a trinket of some sort to represent each of your identities. For example, I used a framed picture of my wife and me sailing around Fastnet Lighthouse to represent Adventurous. For Efficient, I used my business card, as it reminds me that I'm at my most efficient at work. And for Father/King, I used a *khata*, a white Tibetan shawl that one of my friends, a mentee, gifted me to acknowledge me as one of his teachers. It symbolizes embodied presence that provides good, fatherly energy to myself and others.

Once you have chosen your trinkets, place them to one side. Then, as you answer the questions for each of the identities, hold the corresponding trinket in your hand and really take some time to consciously associate with how the words you're using—the sentiments, thoughts, and emotions you're describing—connect with the physical personification of this identity through the trinket in your hand. Take on the body language of what it feels like to inhabit this identity. Notice the emotions you feel, the sensations in your body, and pay attention to your thought patterns while holding this trinket.

What is this identity like when they are at home and at their most relaxed? How do they behave? What do they say? What do they want? What age is this identity? This can range from very young—e.g., "They're still four years of age"—to perhaps a time when you were starting your career. There was a time and place in your life when this part of yourself started to take shape, but this identity, this persona within your ego, may not have really aged beyond that. Or, potentially, they could be a lot older. Maybe they're your current age, though they could as easily be eight, eighty, or eight hundred years old. They might even have a deep wisdom that makes them feel timeless, ancient, eternal. Having various identities with differing ages can help us connect with the multifaceted dimensions of our ego, the parts of ourselves that are seldom examined, that directly impact our leadership and influence.

Here are the headings under which to explore each of your identities:

1. Characteristics
2. Desires
3. Age
4. Emotions
5. Senses
6. Triggers
7. Shadow:
   a. What are they not aware of that the other identities seem to know about them?
   b. What positive aspects of themselves do they shy away from, deny, or doubt?

8. Connections to others:

    a. How do they view and feel about the other identities?

    b. What, if anything, do they want from the other identities?

    c. How do they want to interact with the other identities?

STEP 3. IDENTITY RELATIONSHIPS

Once you've described and explored your identities, bring them into contact with each other to see how they relate.

When you have finished describing all the characteristics of your identities, place each trinket somewhere on the table or floor in front of you, intuiting where they want to go. Which of the other identities are they drawn toward? And which of the other identities want to maintain a distance from them? As we bring each identity into conversation with the other, we get to touch and feel the dynamic components that underpin our leadership presence.

Start by holding one identity trinket in each hand, moving them closer to one another and then farther away. Take on the perspective of one of the identities in your hand, saying what you think of the other one, telling them how you feel, what you want, or how you want your relationship to be from here on in. Then take the position of the other identity, responding to what you've heard, moving closer or farther away depending on the prerogative of this other identity. And then switch over and speak from the other perspective.

You could answer the same set of questions, explain how you feel around the first identity or what you want from them, or make any other statements that arise in the moment. Then pay attention to the answers that come back from the first identity. Do they want to get close to this second identity, or do they want to remain distant? The questions you use are simply prompts, and there's no formula that you should always use; of most importance is that you take your time to do this exercise and really pay attention to any comments, questions, or themes that emerge from the midst of these conversations among your identities.

As you complete each subsequent round of describing and connecting with your other identities, you'll then get to place their corresponding trinket somewhere on the floor or table in front of you. It's particularly important to notice where they sit in relation to each other. For example, as my Father/King identity was placed down on the table in front of me, the other two moved aside to create space for him in the center. This whole process of engaging different identities in conversation together is part of what's called a dialogical approach to the self.[6] Take your time with these conversations, noticing where some identities want to get close to other identities while other identities want to stay far apart.

CONTEMPLATIVE LEADERSHIP AND IDENTITIES

This is an unusual exercise that requires us to acknowledge our cynicism and skepticism, relinquish control, and go with the ebb and flow of this creative process. It's the very epitome of contemplative engagement—whereas the temptation may be to attach and control the process or else disengage and detach from this kind of uncomfortable thinking, a nonattached, curious approach allows us to pay attention to what's coming up for us as we venture outside of our comfort zones. If we seek to replace cynicism, skepticism, or fear with an approach of openness, curiosity, and playfulness, by the end we'll have a sense of which dominant identity, or two dominant identities, tend to be the center around which the others orbit. Some identities will be very similar to each other, and others will be quite different, so learning about their underlying characteristics and motivations can shine a light on the areas of divergence, the bottlenecks, the tensions, and conflicting motivations that fundamentally impact our leadership.

Notice which of the identities help you to access your ventral vagal state, that give you a sense of safety, creativity, and possibility. And notice which of these identities have an underlying narrative that makes you feel stressed or that you need to push to achieve certain things.

The point of this identities exercise is to help us understand the deeper drivers we have. To gain insight into the conscious and unconscious self-images that motivate our very presence, our perspectives, our decisions, and our interactions. Repeating this exercise from time to time can be helpful, especially when we're facing seasons of change, as this allows us to uncover our inner tensions and evolving desires.

Our external environment will inevitably change as we move through different seasons of life. During young adulthood, at the outset of our career, we take on certain roles in our organizations (e.g., a team member or mid-level manager) and in our personal lives (e.g., a committed athlete, a loyal friend, an energetic socialite). And the behaviors we display in these environments emanate from the prominent roles and identities that influence our values and behaviors. But as we mature into different life phases, our identities develop or new identities emerge, which allows us to inhabit new roles as they develop. For example, we enter into committed romantic relationships, parenthood, or a caregiver role for a relative, and our values realign; our behaviors change. We spend time in different ways than we did in the past. We don't value socializing in groups every night of the week.

Or we start a company, receive a promotion into a leadership role, run for office, make a career pivot, or retire out of working life. And whatever new environment we find ourselves in has a trickle-down effect throughout the Logical Levels, impacting our behaviors, capabilities, values, identities, and sense of meaning. But equally, as we lean into these roles and identities, they influence our values, our capabilities, our behaviors, and, ultimately, the people and systems we encounter in our environment. As we face situations in our environment that inspire us to lead, we enact the latent leadership capabilities we have within.

When we begin to identify as a leader, we start to behave as one.

Chapter 7

LEADING WITH MEANING

A life's work is not a series of stepping-stones, onto
which we calmly place our feet, but more like an
ocean crossing where there is no path, only a heading,
a direction, in conversation with the elements.
Looking back we see the wake we have left as only a
brief glimmering trace on the waters.

—David Whyte[1]

Over the last number of years, there's been an explosion of "purpose work" in the corporate world. From consultants like McKinsey and Bain, to corporations ranging from Kellogg to Southwest Airlines to Charles Schwab, having purpose statements and helping organizations discover their sense of purpose has become very important. Of the Fortune 500 companies, 424 have some sort of purpose or mission statement that reminds them of who they are, what they stand for, and, therefore, where they seek to go next.[2] Examples include:

- "To drive human progress through freedom of movement." (Ford Motor Company)
- "To inspire and empower families to lead fulfilled lives." (Kohl's)
- "Connecting People. Uniting the World." (United Airlines)

Whereas some might view mission statements as a cynical corporate exercise that lacks substance, others will see it as a genuine attempt to channel corporate activities that make a meaningful contribution to the lives of their employees, customers, and wider society.

There's nothing new about seeking to derive a sense of meaning from our individual and collective efforts. Over 2,500 years ago, Aristotle was writing about how to live "the good life" that brings a person a sense of deep satisfaction,[3] and about two thousand years ago, Jesus of Nazareth applied some existentialist philosophy when he asked, "What does it profit a person if they should gain the whole world yet forfeit their very self?"[4]

In more recent times, this sense of purpose or meaning in life has taken other forms. Viktor Frankl, a psychiatrist who survived a Nazi concentration camp, wrote a book about his experiences entitled *Man's Search for Meaning*. Frankl went on to create an existential approach to psychotherapy called "logotherapy," which literally means "therapy through meaning." Frankl was influenced by the German philosopher Nietzsche, often quoting his line: "He who has a *why* to live for can bear with almost any *how*."[5] Frankl believed that it was possible to find meaning in all circumstances in life, even the most challenging situations one can face. Readers of his book are asked to reflect on what sustains them in times of challenge. Frankl proposed that we can all find a sense of purpose in everyday life, and he challenged his clients to look for moments of meaning in daily experiences of small sufferings and love, as well as the time spent at work and the humdrum chores of domestic life.[6]

There's something both beautiful and challenging about a survivor of a Nazi concentration camp telling us that it's possible to find meaning in *everything* and that, if we know *how* to look, we can see meaning in the details of every day. Frankl's focus on suffering and our *choosing* to find meaning in our life experiences ties in with another concept that has become very popular in both leadership development and popular psychology over the last few decades: our passions. What is it that we are passionate about?

The word *passio*, from the Latin root, means "a form of suffering that must be endured."[7] Why do we get up in the morning? Why do we go to work? What does our overarching life narrative, our script, tell us about what we deem meaningful? Another way of answering these questions is by examining which of our many identities is most central, most influential, in determining what we're willing to suffer for. Coming to grips with this understanding of what we're passionate about determines the trajectory of our leadership.

TWO APPROACHES TO MEANING

Broadly speaking, there are at least two different perspectives on finding and living with a deep sense of meaning. The first is that there is an objective meaning that we need to *find*. We have one path, one destiny, and any deviation to the left or right is unhelpful, as it moves us away from our unique path. The second is that there is no single meaning for our lives and no single pathway to follow. This perspective moves away from that deterministic thinking, instead focusing on finding meaning in how we *respond* to life as it unfolds. How we respond to each situation reflects our sense of meaning in life and gives us an opportunity to further deepen and develop how we translate that meaning into tangible actions: how we deal with conflict in our team, how we distribute bonuses when our business has a good year, our ability to be present to others in our organization or to appreciate the breathtaking beauty of a memorable sunset instead of scrolling through emails on our phones. The ways we are present to all these different scenarios reflect our capacity to find meaning as life unfolds.

The Greek poet Constantine P. Cavafy beautifully captures the essence of this second perspective of meaning in life with his poem *Ithaka*. It is an homage to Homer's epic poem *The Odyssey*, in which King Odysseus journeys to many destinations, encountering multiple trials and detours in his long passage home from the Trojan War. Odysseus, given the chance, would have gone straight home. But getting back home to his kingdom of Ithaka was made all the sweeter because of the meandering course his life took. Cavafy's poem is an invitation for us to find significance and to see meaning in every moment of our leadership, of our lives.

ITHAKA

> *As you set out for Ithaka*
> *hope your road is a long one,*
> *full of adventure, full of discovery.*
> *Laistrygonians, Cyclops,*
> *angry Poseidon—don't be afraid of them:*
> *you'll never find things like that on your way*
> *as long as you keep your thoughts raised high,*
> *as long as a rare excitement*
> *stirs your spirit and your body.*

Laistrygonians, Cyclops,
wild Poseidon—you won't encounter them
unless you bring them along inside your soul,
unless your soul sets them up in front of you.

Hope your road is a long one.
May there be many summer mornings when,
with what pleasure, what joy,
you enter harbors you're seeing for the first time;
may you stop at Phoenician trading stations
to buy fine things,
mother of pearl and coral, amber and ebony,
sensual perfume of every kind—
as many sensual perfumes as you can;
and may you visit many Egyptian cities
to learn and go on learning from their scholars.

Keep Ithaka always in your mind.
Arriving there is what you're destined for.
But don't hurry the journey at all.
Better if it lasts for years,
so you're old by the time you reach the island,
wealthy with all you've gained on the way,
not expecting Ithaka to make you rich.

Ithaka gave you the marvelous journey.
Without her you wouldn't have set out.
She has nothing left to give you now.

And if you find her poor, Ithaka won't have fooled you.
Wise as you will have become, so full of experience,
you'll have understood by then what these Ithakas mean.[8]

If we approach meaning from a contemplative place of openness and curiosity, of not forcing any particular outcome but being present and nonattached to what is happening within us and in our environment, we can *choose* to find meaning in the situations that we encounter throughout life. This includes times of celebration and times of challenge, and it enables us to lead with inner presence and connection to others, as well as to lead on autopilot, when we feel tired and disconnected from ourselves, just about getting through the day. This approach to meaning allows us to have our "off" days, when we're feeling a little checked out and living in our dorsal vagal state or feeling very stressed in our sympathetic nervous system state. It supports us as we experience great challenges, suffering, and pain, reminding us that this is a natural part of life and that being present to ourselves and others in challenging times is meaningful and deeply important.

We experience suffering any time we are not in control. This can happen when people, organizations, and systems in our lives exert unwanted influence over us: a law is passed that restricts our choices; a leader makes a decision that curtails our opportunities; a colleague stops listening to our input on a project. Or weather affects our travel plans; we experience the bereavement of losing a loved one; somebody perpetrates a crime against us. The suffering can have a physical or a psychological dimension to it, or both. But either way, we suffer because we were not in control. Then there is the suffering that originates from within: we want something that we don't have and can't get: a promotion, a partner, a different lifestyle. Things aren't going according to the plan of our script. Again, we suffer because we are not in control. We are "attached" to certain things happening and other things "not happening," and the degree to which we are attached, to that degree we suffer.

Having this perspective on meaning encourages us as we engage in life from our ventral vagal state, where the light of our identities comes to the fore and we feel present, open, and connected to those around us. It means that we don't have to force situations or take control to lead. Rather than instinctively reacting when situations go in a different direction than what we would have liked, we can instead be adaptable and flexible and choose how we respond internally and engage externally with each person and situation that we encounter. Rather than thinking and behaving from the narrative that says *This shouldn't be happening to me*, we can create meaning in how we respond—in how we lead, in and through each moment.

Fundamentally, this approach of *choosing* to find meaning in each situation and in each conversation, regardless of whether they're ideal, is a profoundly contemplative way of being present to what *is*. Choosing to see meaning in the valleys as well as on the mountain-top requires a radical acceptance of what we're experiencing. We're not wishing something else were happening right now, playing the victim, or otherwise complaining about how unfair this situation is. We are here, in this moment, paying attention to what is happening, noticing how we feel and what we're thinking. And then, fully acknowledging what we're experiencing, we respond from a place of inner depth and presence.

Too many leaders, however, react to challenges by seeking to control as many of the external stakeholders as possible. This often comes from a place of internal fear. When we're afraid of being out of control, we fight tooth and nail to restore any semblance of order we can find in our external environment. We'll leverage our influence through friendly conversations or manipulative interactions, we'll force others to contribute through wounding personal criticism—whatever it takes to get the job done. When we lead from a place of inner fear, we can easily become overly attached to the outcomes we're looking for, doubling down on the tasks we and others need to complete to achieve our goals. But the more we do this in a command-and-control, dominating fashion, the less respect that others will have for us, and the more likely it will be that they'll only do enough to get by, whatever the minimum is that's required. They'll tick a few boxes and do what we tell them to align with the positional power that our role or title requires of them. But our team and organizational culture will struggle. Others won't naturally follow us, talk openly with us, or trust us. And when things get difficult, when we need more work from them, or when we can't dangle the hope of a raise, a bonus, or stock options in front of them, they'll naturally become disengaged, and we and the whole organization will suffer.

But when we face our fears and continue to engage with them on an ongoing basis, when we ask deeper questions about our sense of purpose and meaning and what it is that we are passionate about that propels us forward despite the suffering we'll have to withstand, we are then able to face every life situation, and especially every leadership challenge, with a deep-seated confidence. This confidence is not necessarily that we'll succeed or overcome each leadership challenge we face by getting our own way; instead, it's a confidence that we can engage with whatever comes our way, that we can try and fail and try again. And that our very engagement with each challenge, the very presence that we bring to others involved with us in these challenging situations, combined with the flexibility that comes from a nonattached stance in the world, will enable us to face any challenge with a sense of equanimity and purpose. It is this nonattached, contemplative approach to leadership, thoroughly supported by ongoing contemplative practices as well as a deepening journey into our Inner World, that empowers us to face every situation with both humility and confidence.

A line I often use with coachees is, "We can only lead others as far as we have first gone ourselves." And, in the same way, we can only respond to external challenges with composure and presence on an ongoing basis if we have a sense of composure and presence for the internal challenges we face. We need to continually plumb the depths of our Inner World, accepting who we are so that we can courageously bring the overflow of this inner presence to find and create meaning in the ever-changing Outer World where we lead.

LIFELINE OF MEANING AND THE THREE DOMES OF MEANING

I myself am a question which is addressed to the world, and I must communicate my answer, for otherwise I am dependent upon the world's answer.
—Carl Jung[9]

The purpose of the following two exercises is for us to reflect on some of the life experiences that have shaped who we are. The first exercise, a type of lifeline, charts important moments, experiences, and relationships in our life. The second exercise, called the Three Domes of Meaning, helps us connect these individual experiences of meaning to other people, groups, teams, and organizations.

In chapter two, we completed an exercise around ontology and epistemology, looking at meaning through the lens of the narratives that we've inherited from others. We reflected first on our ontology, the messages we received from our school experiences, the interactions we had in our local community, and the overarching messages unconsciously learned from our society that told us what constitutes "the good life," what was expected *of* us, and what gives us a sense of meaning and purpose in life. Then we examined the epistemology, the sources of authority that taught us that these messages of our ontology were accurate. These sources ranged from role models and people of influence to books and movies, from systems such as religious communities to political institutions on a local, national, and international level. Now we're going to build on that exercise by broadening and deepening the *gestalt*, the whole picture, of what gives us a sense of meaning.

1. LIFELINE EXERCISE

What moments and experiences in life have brought you a deep sense of meaning and purpose? These could be something very fleeting and innocuous, or they could be momentous experiences, peak moments that have stayed with you and others all your life. They might have been high points or low points, or ongoing experiences such as relationships with family members or romantic partners, but what they all have in common is a real sense of aliveness and importance. Here is an example of the moments and experiences that have brought me a deep sense of meaning and purpose in life:

Age:

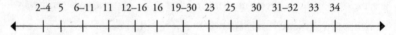

2–4 5 6–11 11 12–16 16 19–30 23 25 30 31–32 33 34

2–4: Time spent with grandparents seemed magical, safe, meaningful—like this was the most important way of spending time. Went on walks to see the trains and down to the beach to see the fishing boats come and go.

5: Prayer times with my mum felt like I was connecting with eternity.

6–11: Class representation, from welcoming visitors to representing my class and school at competitions, taking responsibility, and feeling proud to be selected to represent others.

11: Death of my nana, a deep sense of continuing to prioritize important relationships. One of the most profound, sad, beautiful, and impactful experiences of my life.

12–16: Summers spent on an island in the west of Ireland with friends, speaking Irish and embracing sports and Irish music and culture, helped ground my sense of identity and connect with ancestral heritage. The highs and lows of teenage love.

16: Depression, questioning the value system of my subculture. Chose a life path for myself that was very different from the mainstream teenage agenda of those around me. Sought to value connection with others and within myself, as well as meaningful contributions to others in life. All arose from an experience of depression that led to a profound and unexpected spiritual awakening.

19–30: Series of highs and lows in romantic relationships.

23: Chose to leave management consulting because it didn't resonate well with me at that time.

25: Pursued my dream of aviation and was deeply disappointed to discover I was color-blind. Soul-searching and being reminded of what is most important to me. Difficult journey of recovering from disappointment.

30: Had the courage to turn down the safety of a job promotion to start my own company.

31–32: Encouragement of my now wife to stick at it in my new company, despite so many uncertainties.

33: Giving a TEDx talk.

34: Connecting with a hero of mine; becoming good friends; having healing father-energy in my life.

Now complete your own lifeline exercise of moments and experiences that have been most meaningful for you, and reflect on them by answering the following questions:

Age:

- What are the common themes among the highs?
- What are the common themes among the lows?
- Who and what kept you going when life was tough?
- What are the patterns—the deeper, recurring themes—that emerge as being most important for you?

2. THE THREE DOMES OF MEANING

The Cosmic Egg is a model that I learned from my friend Richard Rohr that he, in turn, adapted from Joseph Chilton Pearce. It traces its origins back to the twelfth-century German polymath and anchoress Hildegard of Bingen, who wrote about her vision of the Cosmic Egg in her book *Scivias*.*,[10] In his interpretation of the Cosmic Egg, Rohr divides the overall cosmos into Three Domes of Meaning that look at My Story, Our Story, and The Story.[11] Each of these Three Domes of Meaning is graphically represented in the shape of three interlocking eggs; the dome of meaning of My Story is the smallest of the three eggs and fits within the next dome of meaning, Our Story, which in turn fits within the largest dome of meaning, The Story. They all link together in a way similar to how stacking dolls fit within each other. These Three Domes of Meaning are very helpful for us as we explore the sense of meaning that we have across all the aspects of our life. Take some time to reflect on each of these Three Domes of Meaning in your own life. Begin by answering the questions that relate to My Inner World (My Story), and then move on to Our Outer World (Our Story) before finishing with The Whole World (The Story).

---

* Many other ancient cultures have depicted the cosmos in some kind of egg-shaped imagery—e.g., the *Hiranyagarbha*, or golden egg of the Hindu Rig Veda texts, and the *Omphalos* stone, the navel of the world according to ancient Greek culture, located at Delphi.

I. MY INNER WORLD

Much of this book has been focused on exploring My Inner World or My Story, asking questions of ourselves such as:

- What are the various identities that we have and where do they come from?
- What values do we hold dear?
- How have we internalized the messages that we've learned from our experiences of challenge and failure?
- What physiological processes take place within our body when we experience stress, exhaustion, and relaxation? And, fundamentally, how we are present to ourselves and to others through each of these experiences?

We have already explored My Inner World in some depth. Taking your insights from previous exercises in the book, and using your answers from the lifeline exercise you just completed, summarize your current understanding of your Inner World in a few bullet points. Then write them onto the Inner World section of the blank diagram on page 158.

II. OUR OUTER WORLD

The next dome of meaning is Our Outer World of meaning, or Our Story. This is where our Inner World encounters and interacts with the Inner World of others. Organizational culture, team culture, and societal and local community culture all form part of this dome of meaning. Our family, our friends, our colleagues, our customers, our clients, and our competitors all fall within this dome as well. When we get along well with people, when we see the world through similar lenses and when there's a lot of overlap in our shared narratives, we can experience tight bonds of shared identity in Our Outer World of meaning. This usually feels good and safe, but it can also develop into a situation of groupthink.

This happens when we become an in-group and we band together with others who easily fit within our way of perceiving reality. When we first connect with others on this level, we usually define ourselves by what we are *not*. This corresponds to the Surviving, Belonging, and Overcoming approaches to leadership that we'll explore in chapter ten. We often regard people who don't follow our lead or who don't see the world as we do as too different or too difficult. We cast them to the periphery of our community, our organization, or our team, and we tend to pay less attention to their opinions and perspectives. We don't fully respect their values and worldviews. In fact, when we are young or when we are part of a community that embraces a binary worldview of things being *either* good or bad, people being *either* for us or against us, these "other" people, communities, and cultures represent worldviews that are so different to ours that they can come to be regarded as everything that we are not and who we do not want to become.

We project our own shadow onto them; we make them the scapegoats of all that is wrong with our own community. Our shadow, as we explored in the identities exercise of chapter six, is all the parts of our personas that we cannot see but that other people are very aware of. And it's also the parts of ourselves that we suppress, that we deny and cover up, often out of fear of our True Self, our capabilities, and our potential. For example, if our shadow is weakness, we might see others as being weak and believe that we, or our teams, need to take control and give clear direction to other, "weaker" teams that we interact with at work. Or, if our shadow is that we dislike how our political party can be "economical with the truth," then we'll work hard to uncover any kind of inaccuracies in other political parties and be vociferous in pointing out their flaws. We project our shadow onto others and become adept at finding fault in the Outer World of individuals and groups who are different from us. This self-deception is a natural overflow of our shadow, a psychological blind spot that we use to avoid facing inconsistencies or areas for development within My Inner World or Our Outer World.

As we mature and develop throughout our lives, it is possible to come to a place of deeper self-acceptance within our Inner World. This might lead us away from being as close as we once were with certain groups in Our Outer World—e.g., as we change and grow, childhood friendship groups or political-party affiliations or college friends might become old-fashioned or distasteful to us. We start wanting to spend less time with these groups and more time with others, even with groups we once thought were strange or very different from us.

On the other hand, our change and growth might even lead us to initiating change within our groups. As others see us grow and develop, they will likely reject us at the start, criticizing us to our faces or behind our backs. But if we continue to display new behaviors that reflect our deepening self-acceptance and stay close to these people we've known for a long time, then our "self-acceptance" can overflow into "other-acceptance." In time, our acceptance can impact everyone around us and, as members of our group become more accepting of themselves and of each other, they will, over time, naturally become more accepting of other groups as well.

Former enemies become compatriots. Our eyes are opened, and we're now able to see what we share, such as a desire to perform, a sense of courage, a passion for certain sports and hobbies, a love for our own families. And we stop dehumanizing different groups as being "other" from us and start to recognize and accept them based on what we have in common. Our Outer World can eventually develop to the point where we respect the stories, the values, and the cultural bonds of other groups even though they will always be different from us. This happens when we transcend the pursuit of dominance, the pursuit of one homogenous group that does things *our way*, and instead come to appreciate and respect other groups despite—and because of—their differences. For example, in his *Harvard Business Review* article on leadership styles, Daniel Goleman mentions six different approaches. These include the Coercive style (a "do what I say" approach), the Authoritative style (a "come with me" approach), the Affiliative style (displaying an attitude of "people always come first"), the Democratic style ("giving everyone a voice" in decision-making), the Pacesetting style (being a trailblazing leader whose high performance motivates others), and the Coaching style (emphasizing the personal development of employees more than "immediate work-related tasks"). Bringing a more contemplative approach into our leadership, we might acknowledge the benefits of, for example, more Coercive and Pacesetting leadership styles that are totally different from our Democratic and Coaching styles and accept that there's a context where that works well—even if we don't want to use it ourselves.[12] Or we might accept that other aid agencies have a totally different agenda, philosophy of development, and means of influencing political power in developing countries and, rather than criticizing or belittling them, acknowledge some of the good work they do. Or we can accept that the Diversity and Inclusion team or the strategy function of external auditors are not totally irrelevant, even if we still don't enjoy working with them—and make a conscious choice to try and aid them in their initiatives and promote them within our own department.

Over time, as we become more accepting of ourselves (My Inner World) and of our groups (Our Outer World), we naturally become more accepting of other groups (Other Outer Worlds) as well.

III. THE WHOLE WORLD

The Whole World represents all that exists, from the interconnected systems of society—including commerce, politics, and religion, global approaches to trade, diplomacy, and technology—to the very existence of our planet within the universe. It is the overarching story, the metanarrative, that encompasses all of the cosmos. In the context of making money, having a meaningful career, living a passionate life, and leading others from a nonattached place of presence and connection, what is the overarching story that we're a part of? It encompasses our collective Outer Worlds, which include all the beauty of human and planetary existence, plus wars, financial crises, pandemics, and climate change.

Richard Rohr calls this dome of meaning "The Story" and writes that it represents "the patterns that are always true" that save "us from the illusion of 'we' and the smallness of 'me.'"[13] For example, "forgiveness always heals; it does not matter whether you are Hindu, Buddhist, Catholic, or Jewish. Forgiveness is one of the patterns that is always true," says Richard. "It is part of The Story (The Whole World). There is no specifically Catholic way to feed the hungry or to steward the earth. Love is love, even if the motivation might be different."[14]

As we consider the sense of meaning that we have in different contexts, we notice that some of us start with the general and move to the particular—the "patterns that are always true." Our experiences of these, such as healing or loving, can begin as an abstract concept that then plays out in the daily life of My Inner World. For others, we begin at the level of Our Outer World, taking our cues from our group identity and subsequently experiencing them in a more personal, intentional way. It doesn't matter which of the Three Domes of Meaning we inhabit to begin with; we can grow into all three domes as we mature across our lifespan.

Take a few moments to look over the diagram on page 157. Seeing the connections between all Three Domes of Meaning is important and helpful, as it allows us to notice the interplay between what is most meaningful for us today and how we can "enact" this deep sense of meaning in the groups, organizations, and global contexts in which we lead.

THE THREE DOMES EXERCISE[15]

1. What is happening in My Inner World right now, at this phase in my life? How has my Inner World developed across the span of my life?
2. How does My Inner World connect with Our Outer World? What are the communities, groups, and organizations I'm a part of today? What communities, groups, and organizations have I been a part of in the past? What Other Outer Worlds—other communities, groups, and organizations—do I acknowledge and respect, even though their stories are different from my own?
3. And then, fundamentally, what is The Whole World story? In the context of the expanding universe, black holes and supernovas, the changing climate of Earth, the evolution of our species, the quality of life for future generations, being a leader in work and outside of work, having a meaningful career, having a sense of fulfillment, and living a passionate life, what is The Whole World story, the metanarrative, that gives me a sense of meaning and purpose?
4. Reviewing some of the key words you wrote as answers to questions 1, 2, and 3 above, write them out in the appropriate dome of meaning in the diagram on page 158.
5. Where are the overlaps across all Three Domes of Meaning, from My Inner World to Our Outer World to The Whole World? What does this tell you about your sense of meaning in how you lead and influence others?

The Three Domes of Meaning

The Whole World
The Story
WHAT IS

The great patterns that are always true

Saves us from the illusions of "we" and the smallness of "me"

My Outer World
& Other Outer Worlds
Our Story
WE ARE

Group identities and loyalties that expand our sense of self

Group ontology and epistemology, our narratives

Nationalism, cultural religion, and philosophy

Ethnicity, groupthink

My Inner World
My Story
I AM

The narrative of my life experiences

My "script" and how I face
challenge and "failure"

My autonomic nervous system states

My values and beliefs

My identities (my personas and their shadow)

My sense of meaning and purpose

**My False Self and True Self all together
(My Whole Self)**

Why I lead

The Three Domes of Meaning

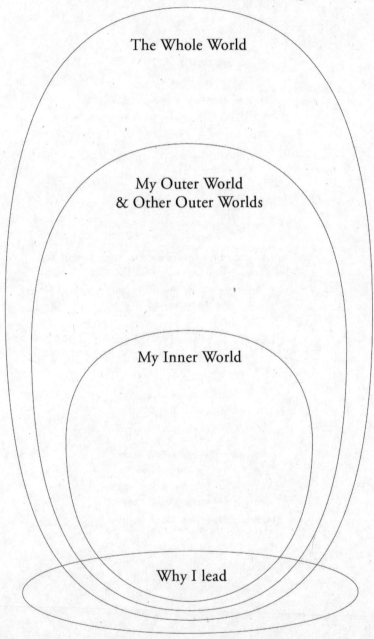

The Whole World

My Outer World
& Other Outer Worlds

My Inner World

Why I lead

Part II

THE OUTER
JOURNEY OF
CONTEMPLATIVE
LEADERSHIP

Chapter 8

INTERPERSONAL RELATIONSHIPS

*How are you complicit in creating the conditions you
say you don't want?*
—Jerry Colonna, executive coach

The movement from our Inner World to Our Outer World is essentially concerned with bringing our nonattached presence into contact with others. Having spent the first section of the book examining the facets of our Inner World that make us the leaders we are today, let's now explore some frameworks that can help us lead others from a place of contemplative presence. We'll first consider the scope of our influence on others and then look at some fundamental communication dynamics before moving on to consider the nature of groups and teams. There are myriad other applications of how to bring our contemplative presence to bear in the relationships and systems within which we lead. Many consulting books and models of team and organizational dynamics are extremely helpful for these (agile methodologies and holocracies are worth exploring). But more than any change model or organizational framework, it's the quality of our presence and our capacity to connect with others to build trusting working relationships that underpins all our leadership endeavors. The chapters that follow serve merely as a starting point to help us connect our contemplative presence to the Outer World of the people and organizations where we lead.

Dr. Robin Dunbar is a British anthropologist and psychologist who is famous for his research into the number of meaningful relationships a person can have. He defines "meaningful relationships" as those with people who "you know well enough to greet without feeling awkward if you ran into them in an airport lounge."[1] He began his research with primates, the result of which posited the idea that there is a correlation between the brain size of a primate and the group size within which they socialize. And he concluded that "the size, relative to the body, of the neocortex—the part of the brain associated with cognition and language—is linked to the size of a cohesive social group. This ratio limits how much complexity a social system can handle."[2] This group size typically ranged from between one hundred to 250 members, with the average number being 150. He applied his research to humans and suggested that, for communities with members who really want to remain close to each other over the long term, this group size of 150 was the most beneficial. Malcolm Gladwell's 2000 book, *The Tipping Point*, discussed "the Dunbar 150" and hugely popularized this theory of an optimal group size required for stable social relationships. Gladwell gave examples of how, through trial and error, companies restructured their operations to have no more than 150 employees in the same building; any more than this, and a string of social challenges arose.[3]

There are many historical and contemporary examples of human communities and groupings organized into sizes of approximately 150 people. These range from Neolithic Middle Eastern village sizes around 6,000 BCE[4] to the size of English villages around the year 1085 CE (as recorded in the Domesday Book[5]), from the size of units in the armies of ancient Rome to the sixteenth-century Spanish army and twentieth-century Soviet army, to Twitter users being able to maintain between 100–200 "stable relationships" at a time. [6,7]

The Dunbar 150 can be graphically represented as a series of concentric circles:

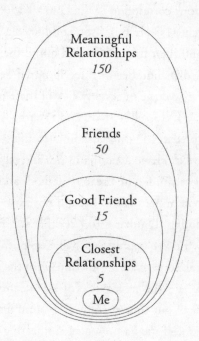

According to Dunbar's theory, the smallest circle, encompassing our closest relationships, is made up of just five people. Then, the next layers of relationship are made up of increasingly larger numbers, with room for fifteen good friends, fifty friends, 150 meaningful contacts, five hundred acquaintances, and 1,500 people you can recognize.[8] There's a fluidity among these expanding circles of relationships, with people coming and going across each of these circles for much of our lives. But if we meet a new person and include them in one of these circles, then we automatically move someone else out of that circle. Two common examples of this are when we move from being single to being in a committed romantic relationship and when we become a parent. We usually sideline at least one of our friends or family members from within our closest relationships circle to prioritize this new relationship with our romantic partner or our new child.

However, there is plenty of other research and other examples of group sizes that don't correspond to the Dunbar 150. Michigan State University researcher Nicole B. Ellison conducted a 2011 study into Facebook users and their friendships and found that while the sample size had a median number of three hundred Facebook friends, they considered an average of seventy-five of these online friends to be actual friends.[9] H. Russell Bernard and Peter Killworth's extensive research, which predates Dunbar's, points to there being 290 people with whom we can have meaningful ties and regularly interact.[10] They used completely different research methods and concluded that a cognitive limit on human group size did not exist.[11]

Crucially, though, Dunbar estimates that we spend 40 percent of our time with the five people that make up our inner circle, and then an additional 20 percent of our time with the ten of our good friends that make up the next circle of our relationships.[12] That's almost two thirds of our time spent with around fifteen people. We can have a huge social media presence, connecting with thousands and even millions of people. We can run teams and organizations with many hundreds or thousands of people. But how influential are these core fifteen or so relationships to our lives and to our leadership? It would be useful to reflect on how we are influenced by these relationships and how we in turn influence these important people in our lives.

Regardless of which number you agree with—150, 290, or anything else—it's worthwhile to create our own unique version of the expanding circles of relationships that we have with others. This helps us take stock of the kinds of interactions we have and reflect on the quality of our relationships across all the different relational circles.

RELATIONSHIP CIRCLES EXERCISE

As we begin this chapter on how to bring our presence to connect with others through meaningful relationship, let's consider who we feel closest to and who is most influential in our life at this point in time. The following illustration of the Dunbar 150 relates to the My Inner World (Me) and My Outer World (from Closest Relationships to Meaningful Relationships) domes from The Three Domes of Meaning model.

1. You may choose to fill out the diagram on page 166 from a purely professional perspective, but I'd encourage you to include your personal life as well. You can choose the number of people in each circle; these can be far more or less than what you see in the diagram. Please fill out the first two circles, Closest Relationships and Good Friends.[13]

2. Now consider your social connections—your friends, those you follow on social media, and those who follow you. This includes all your work-related and personal social media platforms as well as in-person networking groups. Out of all the people you know and interact with, who would you consider to be friends and who would you consider to be meaningful relationships? Write these into the next two diagram circles. (You don't *have* to have 150 names by the end.)

3. Looking at the whole diagram now, with whom would you like to spend more quality time? This may necessitate moving them closer into one of the inner circles of relationship with you.

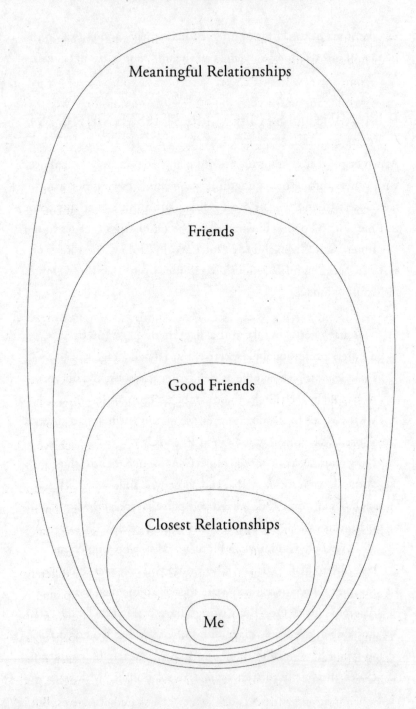

4. Who is currently in one of the inner circles that, if you're honest, doesn't really belong there anymore? To include someone new in that circle, you'll need to move these people into one of your wider circles of relationship. (We unconsciously do this all the time, but making this process conscious may feel a little strange.)

5. What would you like to say to the various people you wish to see move closer or further apart from you? Will you have a conversation or just start behaving differently toward them?

GOALS AND DESIRES

A *goal* is something we want that only requires our input to reach. For example, if I want to get more fit, it's up to me to eat more healthily and exercise more regularly. Or if I want to pass a professional exam, it's up to me to apply myself, to make time to study and learn. I might seek the help of a tutor, but ultimately it's me who'll be taking the exam, so whether I pass or not is entirely my responsibility. A goal is something that I want, that I can aim to achieve on my own, and that has an outcome fundamentally dependent on my direct input. A friend or partner may encourage me in the gym, cook healthy food for me, or even buy my gym subscription, but if I'm not working out properly on a regular basis, no amount of practical or emotional encouragement will assist me in achieving my goal.

A *desire*, on the other hand, is something completely different. A desire is anything that we want that requires the participation or input of at least one other person helping us. There are so many examples of this. Say that one person wants to have an "open working relationship" with another so that they can come to each other with requests for help, with important information and insights, and to collaborate and partner in achieving their shared objectives. But if the other person wants a different kind of working relationship and is assertive about it, saying something to the effect of, "I don't want to work that way," then the first person's desire will not come to pass in that relationship.

Organizational leaders want their clients to purchase an updated IT system, but the clients don't see the need, and now the leader's job is on the line if they can't make their clients change their mind. HR leaders want to introduce feedforward as well as feedback with their colleagues' teams, but if none of these colleagues want to implement this new approach, and if there's no support from the C-suite to force them to, then the well-intentioned desire of the HR leaders simply will not be realized. One person wants to get married, but their partner doesn't feel ready yet.

In each of these scenarios, the healthy approach is to firstly accept that this change is not ready to be made yet. Then, it's time to ask questions, to listen well, to try and understand where the others are coming from, to find opportunities to explain where you're coming from, and to seek real engagement in the process of exploring the potential path ahead—or to discover that there's no chance of having your desires met and to find out what else is required for this relationship.

But often we can confuse our individual goals with these collective desires and become very frustrated and aggressive in forcing our agenda on others. As we become insistent in achieving our desires, our behaviors can turn coercive (using our power to force others to do what we want) or manipulative (such as gaslighting, where we critique the perspective of another person to the point that they start to doubt their own ability to be rational). Or else we passively retreat into the shadows and sulk, taking no further steps toward engaging others or influencing them to discover more about these great opportunities to work together. All these behaviors can fundamentally affect the quality of our relationships and the perceived respect that people have for us as a leader. And the sum of each of these individual interactions will eventually impact the overall culture and direction of our organization.

One of the beautiful elements of contemplation is that it heightens our awareness to what is happening within ourselves as well as to what is happening within others. As we are both present and non-attached to forcing certain things to go our way, we're better able to notice the goals and desires we have. We still *want* these good things to happen—to us, to others, and *with* others—but we don't *need* to force things. There are always other options, other opportunities, if we don't get things exactly the way we want them now. We are that little bit more aware of our ego's deep drive to control Our Outer World. But as we pay attention to our Inner World, we can become more adept at noticing the things we want and the things we *think* we want that are extraneous to our current requirements. Making a distinction between our wants and our needs sounds so simple, yet so few of us do it. It can be profoundly helpful for removing excess stress from our life, for focusing on what's most important and meaningful. For example, in our private lives, we want to borrow money to purchase a car or extend our home, but we may not *need* either of these things. They could just be distractions and stressors that affect our energy for the things we really need, like proper rest or quality time with family and friends.

The same can then be applied to the desires we have for Our Outer World. We learn the energetic difference between a desire whose time has come and is worth investing our energy and leadership influence into and a desire whose time has not yet come, whose very pursuit will distract us, exhaust us, negatively impact the relationships we have, and focus us away from what's most important for us and our organization right now. For example, say we had planned to introduce a new IT system but our latest staff survey shows that there is dissatisfaction around this process; in fact, due to the amount of continuous change over the past years, a sizeable proportion of the team could leave the organization due to burnout. So, now would not be the time to increase workload by beginning another change project. Or say we had planned to spend our allocated budget to run an offsite team-development event on culture and communication, but, due to urgent matters, we've had to shift the dates. We really want the event to go ahead so we can spend our budget before it's taken from us, but these new dates are too close to the financial year end, so it would be extremely difficult for our colleagues and team members to be truly "present" during such a period.

Goals
I have "control"

My actions (processes) alone
determine my goals (outcomes).

Desires
We have "control"

Our relationship: communication,
collaboration & compromise
determine our outcomes.

As we reflect on what we want, over time we become adept at distinguishing our goals from our desires. Then, as we bring our goals into contact with others, we realize that assertively communicating what we want is only the first step in aiming to have our desires met. We need to communicate in ways that allow us to understand the goals of others. And bringing these two sets of goals close together—ours and theirs—provides the basic conditions for us to explore how we might need to compromise, collaborate, and communicate in the pursuit of mutually satisfying desires. A crucial piece here, which can be challenging for us as leaders, particularly if we have positional power *over* others, is to leave space between us and others. For healthy, ongoing relationships to work over the long term, there needs to be a boundary, a space, between where our goals end and someone else's goals begin.

Goals
I have "control"

Desires
We have "control"

My actions (processes) alone determine my goals (outcomes).

Our relationship: communication, collaboration & compromise determine our outcomes.

BOUNDARIES

> *And stand together yet not too near together:*
> *For the pillars of the temple stand apart,*
> *And the oak tree and the cypress grow not in each*
> *other's shadow.*
> —Kahlil Gibran, *The Prophet*[14]

There are entire books written on the hugely important topic of boundaries. I'm using the term to refer to the psychic and energetic space between people, a space that allows every person to be themselves, to have a developed Inner World that they can draw from in how they express themselves in their Outer World of relationships. If we don't have this space, as we bring our Inner World into contact with others in Our Outer World we'll quickly forget who we are, what we think and feel, and what we want. Without this boundary between ourselves and others, we'll take on the wants of others, be overly influenced by the narrative of others, and start to behave in ways that just don't feel like ourselves.

Colleagues or friends will sometimes comment that "You're different when you're with 'those people'" or with "that group." I've coached leaders who talk about how they change in the boardroom or how their spouse or partner no longer wants to attend work dinners with them, as they "act differently" around their colleagues or clients. They're taking on a different identity—"professional," "competent," whatever it might be—and letting their Outer World overly influence their Inner World. Teenagers behave like this when they're around friends, easily succumbing to peer pressure to act in certain ways to fit in. But that's a time in life when their personality is still quite fluid; as adults, especially as leaders, it's important we become increasingly nonattached to the Outer World identities others project onto us and that our presence emerges as an overflow of our Inner World. This is important because, as the famous Asch experiments show, succumbing to peer pressure can continue all throughout our lives, and, eventually, after being exposed to groups of people who have different perspectives from our own, we can begin to question or forget what we "want" and then change our behavior to fit in with the group norm.*, 15 Some of this is helpful and creates the conditions for group identity and team cohesion. But it can become

---

* The Asch experiments on group conformity began in 1951 and have been replicated in many settings ever since. Some versions of the experiments featured seven male college students who were actors and one student who, unbeknownst to himself, was the only real participant in the experiment. The eight students were shown a card with a vertical line and asked to match it to a line of the same length from a selection of three different lines on a new card. During each round of the experiment, most of the seven actors would consistently give wrong answers. The one real participant would initially give the correct answer,

unhelpful if we acquiesce too much, losing touch with foundational identities that inform who we are and what we're about as leaders.

Boundaries

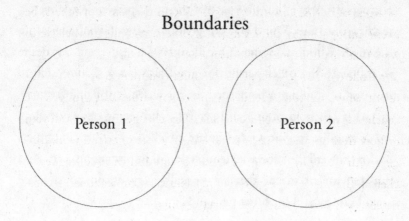

CODEPENDENCE

Without adequate boundaries between us and others, many relationships will veer toward some form of codependence. This is a situation where one person "needs to be needed" (usually a leader) and the other person is "needy." The first person, who needs to be needed, is often competent and capable and can even be very kind. In the best-case scenario, we want to use our leadership capabilities to care for others and help meet their needs, and we have strong ideas around how this should take place. There's a plan, a specific approach, and a clarity of steps as part of an overall process to make things happen.

But even then, we can be so excited by our approach, and so capable of convincing others to follow us, that we can assume that others won't be able to do very much without our direct input. In comparison to us, others can seem less motivated, less capable, and less confident; they need a helping hand.

---

but as the experiment continued, they would begin to conform to the rest of the group and give wrong answers during most rounds of the experiment.

The reality, however, is that if we are this codependent person, with all this energy and focus and capability, we're overextending our personal space into the space of the other person. We're overextending our Inner World and our goals, crossing the boundary into the Inner World of another. Our identity as a leader and our desire to influence the other person for good also has a shadow side to it; we start needing to be needed. In the absence of helping others, investing others in meaningful projects, and seeing others develop, we don't quite feel ourselves. We are attached to influencing others to drive toward the successful completion of important projects. And our attachment means that we—usually very unconsciously—are seeking to control the other person.

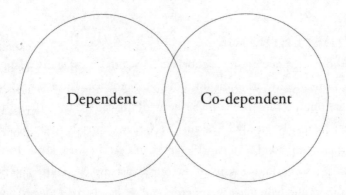

The second person in this scenario is the dependent one. When we are this person, we are needy in some way; we need guidance, encouragement, a plan, or a leader to follow, and without receiving these, we will feel less valuable and less directed. Our communication may default to being passive when we're in contact with the codependent person. Our Inner World may well be explored to some degree, but the gap between our awareness of ourselves and the actions we want to take may be lacking. We might have great insight into our values, identities, and our sense of meaning and purpose, but there's still a ways to go in finding the internal courage to trust ourselves, to speak up, and to exhibit appropriate boundaries with others. We may easily lose sight of our Inner World once we encounter the Outer World of others, especially of this codependent person.

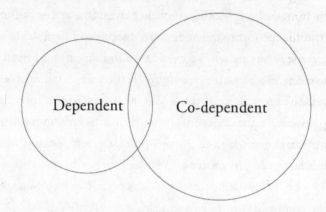

As a codependent relationship develops, we as the dependent person tend to do what we're told, acquiesce to the desires of the codependent party, and generally lose a sense of personal agency in interacting with the other person. We might speak less, trust ourselves less, second-guess ourselves, and generally lose a sense of confidence and capacity to grow and develop over time.

But if we are acting as the codependent party, we will often become more frustrated at the lack of mutuality in the relationship we have with the dependent person. We will take on more and more responsibilities, from simple tasks like checking that emails were sent on time to reading through all of that person's detailed work before signing off and sending it to clients. As the codependent party, we become more directive, take more control, and grow more frustrated at the lack of progress and the lack of responsibility of the dependent person. We begin to think that they are simply "not able to do things" and "cannot be trusted with simple tasks." This becomes a self-fulfilling prophecy, as our taking over more and more tasks from them eliminates their sense of competence and confidence.

We encroach upon the space of the dependent party, disempowering them and creating a dynamic where they rely on us. When this begins, the reliance is often in big areas such as decisions and processes; the dependent party doesn't want to make a mistake, and they want to defer to the experience, wisdom, or confidence of us as the codependent. But over time, that makes themselves smaller, increasingly relying on us for guidance and direction in small things, becoming more passive in communication and less capable of acting based on what they think and what they want. They give over more space to the codependent party and truly become dependent on them in everyday life. At this point, the relationship will lack a sense of equality or mutuality. And no matter how assertive people try to be, subconscious codependent patterns of conversation and interaction will continue to surface.

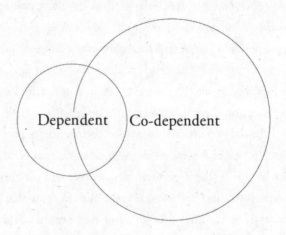

INTERDEPENDENCE

New boundaries need to be established to empower both parties to get some space from each other. And then, over time and with a bit of practice and effort, an interdependent relationship can develop. In this type of relationship, there is adequate space left between the parties; both can find ways to express themselves assertively and to negotiate, compromise, and collaborate toward achieving their shared desires. This might involve, for example, the more organized person taking charge of deadlines and time frames within a project and the more creative person taking charge of design and whatever materials are required. Everyone knows what they are ultimately responsible for; they can each invite the other to make suggestions and express ideas and concerns, but there's a deep sense of mutual respect and an allowing of each other to do what is theirs to do in a manner that makes most sense to them. Suggestions for different approaches don't become opportunities to take control. Frustrations with the other person are voiced on time and with an appropriate level of emotion. Healthy conflict is an ongoing part of communication that takes place within the context of shared responsibility and deep trust.

Interdependence

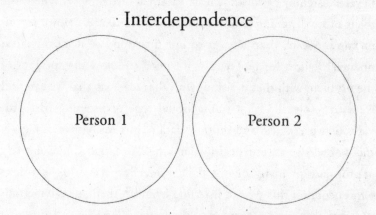

Person 1   Person 2

To move toward interdependence requires a few different relational skills and practices. These include engaging in healthy conflict, finding closure, reestablishing trust, and making new agreements together. But our first steps in developing interdependent relationships is for us to work on our listening presence.

LISTENING PRESENCE

There are many models of listening and approaches to consider when preparing ourselves to really hear from others. The approach that I have consistently found most helpful, because of its simplicity and profundity, is the Three Levels of Listening model that I learned during my executive coaching training.[16]

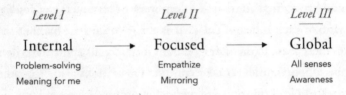

Level I	Level II	Level III
Internal $\longrightarrow$	Focused $\longrightarrow$	Global
Problem-solving	Empathize	All senses
Meaning for me	Mirroring	Awareness

LEVEL I[17]

Level I listening, also known as Internal Listening, is where the focus of my listening is to find out any data that is helpful for *me* to know. We need an answer to our question; we need the latest financial figures for our report; we need to know the specifics of the problem with that division, with that team, so that we can find ways to resolve it. It's a transactional type of listening that provides us with logical and rational data points so that we can apply this knowledge to our decision-making. Although this is entirely appropriate in many of our daily leadership scenarios, if others *only* encounter this type of listening from us, then our interactions together will remain purely transactional. While Level I listening is usually fine for problem-solving scenarios, it does not work for understanding the underlying goals and desires of the other party or for deepening interpersonal connection with them. Stephen R. Covey sums up this level of listening by saying, "Most people do not listen with the intent to understand: they listen with the intent to reply."[18]

LEVEL II[19]

Level II listening, or Focused Listening, is fundamentally different. There is a 180-degree shift in our focus from *me* to *you*. Now our attention is on the person or people before us. What's it like to be in their shoes? How do they view the world right now? What are they feeling? What do they want? We bring a curiosity and a deep empathy to the other. When Level II listening takes place, both parties begin to fall into a pattern of interpersonal congruence. There are many ways of understanding this term, but I mean it to fundamentally describe a situation of mutual co-regulation where we create the conditions for us to each operate out of our ventral vagal nervous system state (from chapter three on polyvagal theory). When we feel safe and connected to each other in this way, we naturally start to mirror aspects of each other's body language. Over time, as our Focused Listening develops into speaking, we'll naturally want to bring an appropriate level of self-disclosure, to communicate that we've heard and really under-stood the other person's point of view. But we will also communicate our own vulnerability and authenticity by sharing something that matches the emotional tenor of the other person.

Level II listening doesn't only happen during deep and meaning-ful conversations on topics of great personal significance. You could just be listening to somebody else express their opinions, their con-cerns, their thoughts, and their emotions on topics related to daily life—a project that they're worried about, a team member that they would really like to see get a promotion. But this focused quality of our listening, which epitomizes a nonattached presence from us, creates the conditions for openness and honesty. And in the process, since we are open to really hearing from the other person, we are also communicating our personal vulnerability, curiosity, and openness to change. Nonattachment in our presence comes across as nonjudg-mental listening. It's a rare gift to give another and a beautiful expe-rience to receive.

LEVEL III

Level III listening, also known as Global Listening, is where we bring our entire presence, all our senses and our awareness, to the person in front of us.[20] This goes beyond curiosity and really hearing from others; it's a commitment to be *with them* as they speak. It's almost as if there are invisible radio waves connecting us, like we know how they're feeling before they speak, as if our intuition knows what they're going to say.[21] This type of listening is by no means typical in everyday organizational life.

People who are in love talk about time standing still, and this results from us being entirely focused on the other person—we know them, and they know us. We're sharing these few moments in time. Poets and mystics describe this awareness as deep knowing. We can find ourselves listening with others at this global level when words are no longer necessary. We are so connected, we so intuit what the other person is communicating, what they want, how they feel, that we can get to the point where neither of us needs to speak. As the thirteenth-century Sufi mystic Jalal ad-Din Rumi wrote, "I closed my mouth and spoke to you in a hundred silent ways."[22] This kind of listening can produce a transformational experience in one or both parties. But it is certainly not always required. In our daily interactions, in the cut and thrust of our leadership influence, our decisions, and the cultivation of meaningful relationships in the pursuit of common desires, Level I and Level II listening will suffice. And for those of us who predominantly operate from within Level I listening, an effort to experiment with Level II can be sufficiently refreshing and energizing for us and everyone else with whom we interact.

As we pay attention to the quality of our presence and listen to others in a focused way, we naturally find a growing curiosity arise from within. *What is happening for them in this moment? How come they made that decision during their meeting last week? Are they operating from a place of fear or courage? From a place of attachment and control? Or from a place of curiosity, nonattachment, and openness to new possibilities and emerging opportunities?*

Listening in a focused way may result in us speaking much less than usual, so when we do speak, our words can carry even more significance. We summarize what we hear as a means of checking in with others, we reflect back the opinions that others express, and we reassure the other person that we're following along and that we're listening to them from a centered place of focus. All of these small details contribute to the other person having a deep sense of being heard. There's a qualitatively marked difference in this kind of listening than in the Internal Listening that most of us experience daily. It usually inspires other people to be more open, to become animated and excited and even quite emotional when they talk. Most of our everyday conversations involve a series of tangents where one person discusses the tip of the iceberg of something important and the other person either explores it with them for a little bit or else springboards away from this important topic to talk about their own experience or something else tangentially related. But Focused Listening creates a wholly different dynamic. We give an opportunity to others to explore their thoughts and emotions, to spend time sharing what's truly important to them. Our presence creates space for others. And our nondirective comments, such as checking in that we're understanding them correctly and summarizing what we're hearing, all continue to offer the other person the freedom to go where they will.

QUESTIONING

At a certain point, it's appropriate and helpful to ask some questions. We want to find out more, or we want to help the other person break their repetitive cycle of finding, for example, more and more ways to express frustration, fear, or doubt. Asking a few key questions can help "unstick" someone who is spiraling into unhelpful thinking, and it can move us all forward to focusing on what's most important to discuss. The key here is to ask open-ended questions that give scope and freedom to the other person to further explore the multifaceted dimensions of their thinking. These questions begin with words like "what," "how," "where," "when," and "who."

The questions that begin with "what" and "how" are, in my experience, the most helpful to use on a regular basis. In training coaches, we often practice exercises where the coach can only speak by asking "what" and "how" questions. These questions make the other person think, going broader and deeper in their reflections and explorations, and can uncover something new in their thinking as well as in their felt emotions. If there's nothing else that you take from this chapter, I'd urge you to combine your Focused Listening with the use of these two simple, powerful questions: "What?" and "How?"

Open-ended questions could include:

- What did you want to see happen at that meeting?
- How did you feel when your colleagues accepted your proposal?
- Where were you in the pitch when the client interrupted you?
- When do you want to revisit this difficult conversation with your boss?
- Who else needs to know about this idea?

When asking questions, it can be tempting to stack them, to ask a few questions at the same time. For example, "Who else knows about this? What will you do next?" Asking more than one question at a time, however, is confusing and usually leads to the other person answering the final question first. They often forget, or just ignore, the other questions. Even the best media interviewers, executive coaches, and psychotherapists are known to make this mistake on occasion. But as we pay attention to what we say, and as we focus on the most important questions to ask, over time we become adept at just asking one question at a time and then giving the other person all the space they need to run with that.

Questions beginning with the word "why" are generally to be avoided as, no matter how innocuous and gentle they may be, or how soft our tone of voice and our body language as we ask it, it's common for "why" questions to sound judgmental. "Why did you decide to go with that supplier?" "Why did you ask them that question?" "Why do you want to take your vacation then?" These questions can provoke a defensiveness from the other person, feeling the need to defend themselves in their words or in their thoughts.

To avoid this sense of judgment while also engaging our curiosity, the occasional question beginning with "how come" can be a suitable substitute. "How come you chose that supplier?" "How come you went with that question?" Though there is very little difference between "why" and "how come" in these examples, there can be a subtle, emotional, and energetic shift that makes it more palatable, coming across as curiosity more than judgment.

The other type of questions to be used with restraint are closed questions. In courts of law across many jurisdictions around the world, closed questions are regarded as leading questions that point to a "yes" or a "no" answer, thus giving less scope for the respondent to explore their thoughts or to explain themselves. For example: "Did you hear what happened at that meeting?" "Do you think that's right?" Or, in certain parts of the world with a unique local syntax: "Do you not think we should go ahead with this strategy?" These closed, leading questions communicate more about the opinion of the interlocutor and give less scope to the respondent to reflect, to riff, or to remonstrate. If we regularly use closed and leading questions with our colleagues, they will feel like we don't really value their expansive thoughts on these topics. This will lead toward very one-sided conversations where we'll either feel that our insights are going unchallenged or else live with a false sense of security, believing that our colleagues are entirely of our way of thinking.

REFLECTIVE EXERCISE

- Returning to the opening Dunbar 150 exercise, identify the three relationships from within your concentric circles that are currently most pivotal for your capacity to lead effectively:

  1.
  2.
  3.

- Journal how your goals and your desires impact each of these three relationships.
- What are the conversations that you really want to have with these people regarding your desires that directly impact them (i.e., you need to enroll them to collaborate or compromise in some way for your desires to become reality)?
- What open-ended questions would you really like to ask them? Write down at least ten questions and then select the top two or three that could potentially open up your conversations.
- How can you prepare yourself to listen in a focused way and to bring a nonattached presence to these conversations?
- Go and have at least one of these conversations before beginning the next chapter.

Chapter 9

CONNECTED
TEAMS

I think I've reached a new level of resilience through
understanding versus resilience through strength or
hardness.
—Matthew McCarthy, former CEO, Ben & Jerry's

DEVELOPING A TEAM

What images come to mind when you hear the word "team"? Memories of your favorite sports teams performing at an exceptional level? Inspiring managers and team leaders that brought a group of disparate individuals together to achieve greatness? Perhaps you were part of a team that left a lasting impact on you, where individuals worked extremely hard and found common purpose with others, collaborating and compromising to achieve something extraordinary together. Or does the word "team" conjure up images of a different nature entirely, something more akin to what many people experience: frustration, power dynamics, lack of clarity, wasted time in discussions, individual efforts not being recognized, and overall dysfunction?

In the 1960s, the psychological researcher Bruce W. Tuckman published his famous work on the theory of group dynamics.[1] He proposed that there are four distinctive phases that groups typically follow as they work together over time. This starts with Forming, then moves on to Storming, which develops into Norming and, finally, Performing.[2] In 1977, in conjunction with the psychological researcher Mary Ann Conover Jensen, Tuckman added a fifth and final phase to the group dynamics model: Adjourning.[3] This reflects the importance of groups of individuals, developed into a tight-knit team, taking some time to consciously unravel some of the bonds and interdependencies that they develop while working together. These five sequential phases became known as the Orming Model (as most of the phases end with the letters "-orming") and, although it has been critiqued and updated in many ways since it was first introduced, it remains a foundational group- and team-development model for leaders and their teams.[4] As we briefly look at each of the five phases, reflect on your own experiences of team dynamics, especially when you were particularly attached to being in control or to forcing specific team results. Recall times when you experienced these phases at work or in your personal life:[5]

1. Where did you thrive?
2. Where did you tend to get stuck?
3. What have you learned about your contributions toward creating a healthy team dynamic?

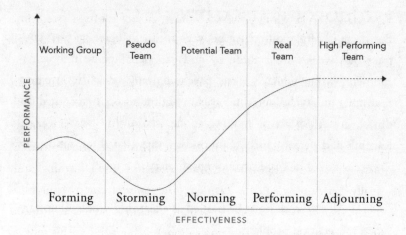

1. FORMING

During the initial Forming phase, groups are often polite and some-what reserved with each other. Some individuals might be anxious or excited—or both—as they form initial impressions of what it will be like to work together. Thinking back to our Three Domes of Meaning, this Forming phase is one where a lot of Inner Worlds encounter other Inner Worlds in the Outer World container of the team. Certain identities come to the fore more than others. The ways we assertively communicate or not, the quality of our listening, the interpersonal dynamics of interdependence or codependence—all impact our experience of this Forming phase.

Choosing specific activities for teams to get to know each other and start building psychological safety can be helpful in this forma-tive stage of team interactions. Teams benefit from explicitly creating a team contract together, clarifying the parameters of their working boundaries, and focusing on what to strive for together.

PSYCHOLOGICAL SAFETY

But there is a huge difference between mutually agreeing on a contract that we *say* we'll abide by and experiencing the right environment within which we feel psychologically safe. The foremost researcher on psychological safety, Amy Edmondson, first coined the phrase in a 1999 article looking at the relationship between team learning and performance.[6] Edmondson says that three conditions are necessary to increase psychological safety in a team:

1. All the work must be framed as a learning problem, not an execution problem
2. Leaders must admit their own fallibility
3. Leaders need to model curiosity by asking a lot of questions[7]

The context in which leaders operate today, according to a recent McKinsey study, suggests that 89 percent of US employees believe that psychological safety in the workplace is essential and that it is the "responsibility of business leaders to create a safe and respectful workplace."[8] If this really is the case, it means that any time we gather in groups, the presence we bring and the tone we set is most essential in creating an environment where we can all thrive. Engaging in regular contemplative practices and self-regulating into our ventral vagal state (e.g., using the "sigh, stretch, smile, touch" and "people, activities, places, times" exercises) creates the conditions within that enables us to co-regulate others. This is the physiological foundation of contemplative, nonattached presence that helps us role model these three conditions of psychological safety.

FRAME WORK AS A LEARNING PROBLEM, NOT AN EXECUTION PROBLEM

This ties in with research on growth mindset, where we bring our curiosity and a sense of playfulness to the problems and challenges we face. With practice, we can move from the narrative that tells us, "We need to get this right" (which focuses on execution) to instead look at challenges with the narrative of, "We need to be present, open, and curious, and we need to ask questions, listen, hear from each other, and find out—from our real-time, lived experiences together—what is working and what isn't." The ways we interact *together*, the processes we choose, can enable us, over time, to move from a working group toward a real team. When a leader invites us to participate on an equal footing, asks for our perspective and ongoing contribution, our engagement levels soar. We feel like we are a part of something bigger than ourselves, and this sense of belonging that ensues draws on our deepest desires to make a difference—together.

ADMIT FALLIBILITY

Many of us grew up in contexts where family members, teachers, and other authority figures hardly ever admitted when they were wrong. So, when somebody did admit a mistake, it likely had a profound effect on us. The ability to admit fallibility displays humility. We admit that our idealized self, our hope of always being correct, is just not possible. We're not hiding our mistake, we're not pretending to be right, and we're not blaming others for feeding us bad data. We're displaying that there's still more to learn. In essence, we're saying, "I may miss something . . . here's what I *think* I know, and please help me fill in any gaps I may have." This is powerful from a leader, as it shows others that it's okay to make a mistake.

MODEL CURIOSITY

And the fact that we don't stop there, that we don't hang our head in shame or feel embarrassed about our mistake but continue looking for the next lesson to learn, displays a positive approach to growth. One of the facets of a growth mindset that can feel strange to some people is to continue to ask more questions and continue to try out new options every time we make a mistake. But our trying again belies our attitude of curiosity, of wanting to change our approach, to ask a new question, to try something else that might just be what we're looking for to address this latest challenge. As we model curiosity, again, we are role modeling a nonattached openness to how we lead. We are implicitly giving others permission to do the same—to ask questions, to try new approaches to resolve old problems, to be interested in discovering more.

In combination with admitting fallibility and treating everything as a learning problem, modeling curiosity is a powerful example to set, giving a vision to the other team members of how they, too, can behave. It gives a snapshot of what might be possible if everyone comes together as an interdependent collective, a team.

2. STORMING

During the Forming phase, most people are "nice" to each other. But as differences in working styles, personalities, and expectations emerge, people start to challenge each other, directly and indirectly. Our identities clash as each person attempts to establish themselves within the team. Though it often begins slowly, this can quickly accelerate to significant conflict. Anyone who can keep their cool, communicate their issues with a balanced assertiveness, and listen nonjudgmentally to others becomes a role model for the entire team of what healthy conflict could look like for all.

It is important that team leaders display an appropriate level of vulnerability during this phase, again showing that they are not perfect and that they don't have all the answers. This is best followed up by the team leader's role modeling of healthy conflict among the team or even by inviting externs to facilitate conflict resolution, which would allow the team leader to more fully participate themselves.

The team needs to discuss conflict and agree on an approach to dealing with it each time it occurs. As conflict comes to be recognized as a normal part of healthy relationships, some of the fear, upset, anger, and reactivity that most of us experience during conflict can be replaced by an openness, and even a sense of calm, as differences are highlighted and addressed.

But before we get there, it is usual for team effectiveness to really drop during this phase of team development. The end of the Storming phase and the beginning of the Norming phase are often quite messy, and it can be difficult to distinguish between where one ends and the next one begins.

During this phase of team development, it is important to start to develop norms in team meetings that encourage a balance of speaking up and letting others speak. Once norms of conflict have been established, the team will usually have to slow their daily pace of work to spend more time building a common understanding of their workflow. This helps map out the overall process of work so that they can make better decisions together as the pace increases into the future.

3. NORMING

The establishment of clear team roles often heralds the beginning of the Norming phase. Team members have worked through their most significant conflict, have agreed to certain behavioral norms, and know how to organize themselves around the work. In some contexts, where the organizational culture encourages it, team members might even begin to socialize together.

During this phase, everybody participates in team meetings. The team begins to reflect on their work, deciding what should be prioritized in their backlog and how they can improve their processes and goal setting for the future. Employee satisfaction, customer satisfaction, and other delivery metrics can all be used in a meaningful way to decide what to change and what to keep from the current way of working. Team members begin to constructively use feedback and feedforward with each other. A degree of trust has been established among the team.

As leaders, this phase helps clarify the reasons we are leading and the relevance of the approaches we have chosen. We might realize that our approach to leadership needs to evolve to match the changing needs of our team. Our abilities to adapt, to be nonattached to our hitherto successful approaches, and to embrace a new approach are critical. This may require shifts to our internal narrative, the My Inner World story of what we hope for from our leadership.

4. PERFORMING

Performing happens when the team is clear about what to do and how to do it. Team members support each other in the pursuit of their shared vision and seek to set and surpass new goals. They will seek and be given higher degrees of autonomy than before. They will be experienced enough to begin achieving mastery in their role, and some will have a growing realization of a sense of meaning and purpose and how it applies to their work. When team members are paid fairly and given some meaningful autonomy in what they do and how they complete their work, they begin to perform at a high level.[9] And if they have enough experience and a long enough track record to feel confident in their capabilities, they will embody a sense of mastery that makes them ready and able to meet whatever challenges come their way.[10] With these two conditions of autonomy and mastery in place, combined with a sense of team togetherness and an ability to engage in helpful conflict, the team now has a deep sense of meaning and purpose that empowers them to do their best work.[11]

5. ADJOURNING

High-performing teams achieve exceptional results because they are so used to their team interactions that they intuitively and implicitly understand what to expect from each other. Their track record of results feeds their confidence. Teams like this have embraced a growth mindset, as they expect that the excellent processes and interactions they have established will inevitably manifest as excellent results.[12] But even high-performing teams do not last forever, and, at some point, either the goals or the team members will change.

It is crucial that the team does not rush this final phase of working together; instead, they need to decide how they want this process of closure—of team Adjourning—to take place. Many teams don't take the time to appreciate what they have achieved together, to say goodbye, and to support each other in moving on to other endeavors. This can be an emotional experience, and it's important that team members celebrate together and reflect on their learnings as they go on to join other teams.

CONTEMPLATIVE LEADERSHIP IN TEAM FORMATION

For some of us, there's nothing new in going through these team-building phases; we've been through them a lot and referred to this model before. And we've sometimes experienced the model in a different phase order: e.g., a new team that immediately begins with conflict, so Storming comes first. But of most importance for our consideration is how attached we are to the team working out. How much control do we need to have? Do we try to force our teams to come together, to move through the Storming phase too quickly, to pursue the upside of growth without giving enough time for the challenges to be laid bare? As is a natural tendency for many, we are so focused on fixing and solving and constructing something anew that we don't allow adequate time for deconstruction and the expression of conflict. If we view the Tuckman model as something too linear and predictable, we can easily focus on the outcome of getting to high performance rather than on the process of getting there.

In my experience of working with teams, very many of them get stuck at the Storming phase. Typically, one or more team members become overly attached to forcing things through while most of the rest of the team moves progressively toward detachment as their opinions, ideas, and desires for the team are disregarded or openly rejected without good cause. It is the reason why so many teams spiral in this Storming phase and don't progress to Norming and beyond. The catalyst that's required to make a significant change is for at least one of the team members to come to the Storming phase with a contemplative presence. This nonattached presence happens when we become aware of the narrative we are attaching to (e.g., "This team should *only* communicate in person or on certain media" or, "We *need* to achieve these three strategic priorities") and choose to let go of it—no longer *needing* that narrative to come true exactly the way we envision. To want the very best yet hold our expectations loosely. To see beyond our individual preferences and needs and instead be open to something different emerging through interacting with the narratives, preferences, and needs of the rest of the team and with other stakeholders beyond the team as well. As leaders become nonattached, we will sometimes compromise, often collaborate, and seek to find common ground with the narratives of others. We practice Focused Listening and have an open presence that gives permission to others to express themselves. Most fundamentally, we are not trying to rush through the Storming phase to quickly arrive at the Norming phase of team dynamics. We are wise enough to realize that the most helpful outcomes emerge out of good processes, and good processes tend to take time.

TRUST

One of the most helpful ways I have found to work with teams stuck in this Storming phase is to focus on their relationships with each other through the lens of trust. A popular understanding of trust, from the columns of agony aunts to the comments of social media posts about "what a person should do" when trust breaks down, is that trust is a binary construct; you either have it or you don't. The 2000 movie *Meet the Parents* features a memorable rendition of this take on trust. Jack Byrnes, the father-in-law-to-be, played by Robert De Niro, continually refers to the "circle of trust" throughout the movie. When the son-in-law-to-be behaves in ways that De Niro's character approves of, he is happily embraced as being within the "Byrnes family circle of trust." But when he behaves in ways that displease De Niro's character, he is told in no uncertain terms that he is "no longer in" that circle. As the plot unfolds, we see the character of the son-in-law, played by Ben Stiller, moving in and out of this circle of trust. Three quarters of the way through the movie, he's emotionally spent, not sure where he stands in relation to De Niro's character. He initially jumps through every hoop placed in front of him, but after a while, he stops caring and actively makes choices that ensure he remains outside of the circle that is, essentially, owned and controlled by someone else. It's a funny movie and a very accurate depiction of how so many of us interpret trust in our personal and professional relationships.

If we see trust as a binary construct, we, too, will experience the fear and frustration of wondering if we're "in" or "out," or else we'll be tempted to wield trust as a weapon, controlling and manipulating the behavior of others to make sure we have our way. This "in or out" approach is not relationally healthy, often leads to poor boundaries and unhelpful communication dynamics, and is an overall very attached way of relating to others wherein we're trying to control the relationship in some way. We end up operating from our sympathetic nervous system state of fight, flight, or fawn, becoming vigilant in our interactions, not feeling very safe.

Much research has been conducted regarding the nature of trust: in defining its various facets, some have said that trust is "the extent that a person believes another person to be benevolent and honest,"[13] while others write that "trust begins where prediction ends," pointing to its very essence being the placing of our faith in another person or system.[14] Different researchers point to trust as being a multifaceted, nonbinary concept,[15] and that relational trust has three components:

1. Predictability: How predictable will somebody's behavior be as we continue to interact with them over a period?
2. Dependability: Can they be "trusted" to do what they say they'll do?
3. Faith: At a deep interpersonal level, are they "for me"?

Building on all this research, and inspired by a model I learned from a phenomenal psychologist friend of mine, Jim McNeish,[16] the following model and its applications of "action and closure" can help teams develop trust, especially when they're stuck in this Storming phase:

LEVELS OF TRUST*

Level of Trust	Characteristics	Is this level of trust intact between me and the other person(s)?
Level 1: Able	Do I trust that this person is able to do the job they've agreed to do? For example, do they have the training to complete a complex/technical challenge? Or can they delegate to others to help organize a large event?	Yes/No
Level 2: Timely	Do I trust that this person will show up to meetings on time or that they will send me an update when they said they would?	Yes/No
Level 3: Honest	Given the professional context, restrictions on information flow, and other appropriate boundaries, do I believe that this person is communicating as openly and honestly as they possibly can with me?	Yes/No
Level 4: "For me"	Do I trust that this person is supportive of me, that they are "for me," on a personal basis? Do they want to see me thrive and be at my very best, or are they trying to undermine or sabotage me in some way?	Yes/No

---

* This Four Levels of Trust table has been adapted, with permission, from the work of Jim McNeish.

It's unusual to have all four trust levels intact with another person at the same time. I've very rarely experienced that myself or seen it at play in the professional or personal relationships of others. The key for us is to move from an idealized, "in or out," binary notion of trust into a multifaceted one that allows us to continue to work with people and relate to them, even when we don't fully trust them in everything.

For example, I have worked for long periods of time with different people where there were consistently two levels of trust missing in our relationship. In one case, I strongly believed that this person was "for me" (Level 4 trust) and their communication with me was consistently open and honest (Level 3 trust). But they were regularly breaking their promises, not replying to emails on time and not preparing adequately for our work together (Level 2 trust). I found this frustrating and often addressed this with them. They tried harder and sometimes made progress but usually dipped back into old habits. On top of this, the more time we spent working together, the less interested they became in developing their core skills and capabilities. This was reflected in their performance and in our shared work. Again, we discussed this, and I mentioned that Level 1 trust was no longer in place, either—I'd lost confidence that they could "produce the goods." This led to an interesting conversation where they admitted to themselves and then to me that their heart was no longer in the work they were doing. Shortly afterward, we stopped working together but stayed in touch on a more personal level. There was no complete resolution, and our levels of trust continued to be as imperfect as they always are in relationships, yet our friendship could continue in another guise.

Another person I worked with had a completely different profile. They were hugely capable at their job and always showed up to meetings well prepared and in good time. Levels 1 and 2 trust were in place, and it was powerful working together. However, they could also be somewhat deceptive when it suited them. I was slow to learn this, hearing rumors from others behind their back, but eventually experienced bald-faced lies to my face. When challenged, they became disproportionately defensive; I had clearly triggered something deep within them. After a cooling-off period, we had a few conversations about the nature of our working relationship and how we would seek to work together moving forward. But in time, the hiding of information and deception around the full truth returned. Given our roles, we had to continue to work together, and, based on my previous experience, it seemed that direct confrontation would do more harm than good. So, instead, I decided to develop much stronger boundaries with this person—to not give away any more information than needed, to critically assess the veracity of their communications, and to pick my battles rather than engage in long-term conflict. When our environment was buoyant, we worked well together, as they were in great form and usually honest. But when our working environment became challenging and they became stressed, their propensity to deceive would return, and I would have to adapt my approach to the relationship to be a little more discerning in my interpretation of what they were telling me.

Over the course of our working relationship, it also became apparent that this person was neither interested in my personal life nor in seeing me thrive and be at my very best (Level 4 trust). But given the challenges we had in our communication and the fact that Level 3 trust was also not intact, I didn't really mind that this person wasn't "for me." Again, it just meant that I had very firm interpersonal boundaries with this person and that most of our conversations were focused on work.

There are many other implications for the outworking of this multifaceted approach to trust. For example, if somebody is always late at delivering their work, but we know that they are "for us" and have the technical abilities to complete the task, then we can trust them with supervised work and aim to develop the other levels of trust. Or, if somebody doesn't respond to emails on time and we real-ize that they are not doing their work, but we know that when asked a question about it they will be open and honest in their response, then we can still maintain a relationship with them and find out what support, training, or delegation they might need us to arrange for them.

CLOSURE

Once there's a breakdown in any of the four levels of trust, some-thing needs to change so that we can effectively work together in the future. Sometimes the only thing we can do is accept that some levels of trust will not be in place.

Level of Trust	What's required to restore a breakdown in trust?
Level 1: Able	Take new actions, try different approaches
Level 2: Timely	Take new actions, try different approaches

If the breakdown in trust is in the first two levels, then we'll need to find new approaches to practical steps we can take in work-ing together—anything that will improve communication and our ability to complete tasks. If these new steps don't work, then we'll have to find workarounds, deleting or delegating some tasks, or else moving people in and out of roles that are most suited to them. New actions are required to restore and further develop trust between everyone. For example, the person I used to work with who was regularly late with work started to make a huge effort to be on time, and many months of our one-to-one meetings then focused on their delivering higher-quality work. But over this time, as they reflected on their ability to do the work, they realized that they weren't quite as interested in it as they first thought. They chose not to complete further professional-development courses and eventually left the role and worked in another sector. Crucially, our relationship was intact throughout that process as I asked for more effort and they leaned in and did their best—before realizing that, deep down, they wanted a different job altogether.

A breakdown in trust at Levels 3 and 4, on the other hand, requires a different approach. When we feel people are not telling us what they know or are being deceptive with the facts, it can leave us with a personal wound. Conscious and unconscious thoughts such as, *Why would they not tell me?* or, *Am I not important enough for them to be open with me?* can emerge from within. Whereas Levels 1 and 2 are concerned with more transactional levels of trust, here we're facing trust at a deeper interpersonal level of relationship. A breakdown in Level 3 trust has the power to offend and upset, and a breakdown in Level 4 trust can feel like outright rejection. It can seem like this person is fundamentally against us; they do not have our best interests at heart; they are not "for us." Ironically, in so many examples I've encountered and even experienced myself, the "guilty" party who has broken the trust of the other person is often unaware that there's been any breakdown in trust at all. If we've experienced this breakdown, then it's our responsibility to address it assertively. We need to pursue a path of closure so that the relationship has a chance to heal and develop.

Level of Trust	What's required to restore a breakdown in trust?
Level 3: Honesty	Seek closure and then redefine the relationship
Level 4: "For me"	Seek closure and then redefine the relationship

According to Sylvester McNutt, "Closure happens right after you accept that letting go and moving on is more important than projecting a fantasy of how the relationship could have been."[17] When we feel betrayed, we often return to our sympathetic nervous system state. Our emotions and hormones can be all-consuming, urging us toward fight, flight, or fawn behaviors. Taking some time for a state change, for a cooling-off period, can be important so we don't rush into doing anything rash. Then, when we're feeling a little less triggered by the situation, we can approach it with a degree of equanimity and nonattachment.

ASSESSING THE BREAKDOWN IN TRUST

The following questions are helpful for understanding how a breakdown in trust has affected us. This is a crucial first step before we can pursue a path of closure, healing, and relational development.

1. In what ways have we been disappointed or hurt by the other person?
2. Have they used their positional role of seniority as an excuse to not listen to me or to disregard my input?
3. Have they misunderstood me and assumed I had different intentions to what were communicated?

4. Were they being guarded in their communication toward me, not open or honest to the extent that they could have been?

5. Does this breakdown in trust remind me of previous experiences with this person? Or is it triggering for me because it reminds me of previous issues I've had with other people?

6. Overall, do I feel disappointed by their lack of interest in me as a person?

For relationships among team members to move forward, it's important to sit with the impact of the breakdown in trust and then communicate how we feel to the other person. But given the neurological wiring we have as humans, expressing criticism at all—even when it's coming from a person who's calm and measured in what they're saying—usually produces an initially defensive reaction. For this reason, any time I'm facilitating sessions on the Storming phase, trust, or closure, I tie in positive feedback.

POSITIVITY IN RELATIONSHIPS

The neuroscientist Rick Hanson coined the "Velcro and Teflon theory of mind" to refer to the negativity bias we each have.[18] Good news disappears from our consciousness as fast as butter slides off a hot Teflon frying pan; bad news, on the contrary, stays with us in the same way that the two sides of Velcro stick tightly together. He summarizes the reason for this when he writes, "As we evolved over millions of years, dodging sticks and chasing carrots, it was a lot more important to notice, react to, and remember sticks than it was for carrots. That's because—in the tough environments in which our ancestors lived—if they missed out on a carrot, they usually had a shot at another one later," Hanson explains. "But if they failed to avoid a stick—a predator, a natural hazard, or aggression from others of their species—WHAM, no more chances to pass on their genes."[19] This means that we are wired to be vigilant for negative feedback. And if someone expresses a breakdown in trust that they've experienced from us, despite our initial defensiveness, most of us will really take this negative feedback to heart. Which, in turn, has the capacity to further worsen the relationship before it has a chance of getting better.

Research from the Gottman Institute points to us needing a ratio of five positive interactions to one negative interaction just to maintain a sense of balance in our relationships.[20] And Hanson goes on to say that, given our negativity bias, we must consciously hold on to a positive feeling or thought for a minimum of fifteen seconds—and ideally thirty seconds—if it is to create a positive imprint in our brain cells and our emotional state.[21] So, a helpful way of enhancing conversations with others around breakdowns in trust is to have a list of all the positive aspects we appreciate about the other person, which we can share with them after we've talked about our perception of the breakdown.

TRUST-APPRECIATION TEAM EXERCISE

The table on pages 206–207 outlines an exercise to address all of this within teams. The context is that everybody has already spent some time focusing on their presence and their quality of listening. Then we look at the "-orming" model and complete some geographical voting exercises around team dynamics—expressing where we're at, what behaviors we experience from others, and what we would like to see change. We then explore barriers to change and see the pivotal role that trust plays in our team and begin to look at how relationships need to change for the team to move forward. Then each person takes some time to complete the worksheet on pages 208 and 209 for each of their teammates, and we start having one-to-one conversations with each other. The first person spends ten minutes talking through all the columns in the worksheet, and the other person simply listens without comment, attempting to really hear what's being said. Then they immediately swap roles and repeat the exercise. It's a challenging activity, but when completed in a safe environment, it's *always* easier than what people expect it to be.

REFLECTIVE EXERCISE

Read the worked-out example on pages 206–207 before completing your own worksheet.

Now reflect on the relationship you have with somebody in your life, whether in your role as a leader or elsewhere, and complete the worksheet on pages 208–209 in preparation for a conversation around trust and further deepening your relationship into the future.

NAME OF PERSON: TJ

Levels of Trust	Examples	Desire for Our Relationship in the Future	What Do I Appreciate About Them?
Level 1: Able	Yes, you're very good at your job and regularly do excellent work.	Continue using the same processes that deliver excellent results.	• Your confidence, great qualifications and experience, and ability to adapt your approach when we're working on different projects with clients who have very different needs. • You're easygoing in team meetings yet sharp and insightful about future projections. Your body language is very open, and you smile a lot, especially when we're meeting new clients for the first time; this makes me and clients feel comfortable and trusting toward you.

Level 2: Timely	Sometimes you're late for meetings and send work through at the last minute.	I'd like us to mutually agree when work is due and for you to commit to those deadlines.
Level 3: Honest	You are usually good at keeping in touch. But when work is late, you stop answering my calls and emails, and I don't know what's happening or when to expect anything.	I don't mind if things are going "wrong"; we can always work together if you're struggling. But I'd like to have real-time updates on your progress, as this also affects my work.
Level 4: "For me"	I'm not sure. Sometimes I don't think you're "for me"—like when you ignore my emails, as this really impacts my ability to do my job, my career, and my enthusiasm as your team leader. I'm confused on whether you're "for me" and would love to discuss this further.	As we communicate more consistently and on time by email, by phone, and in person, I'd like to get more of a sense of your support for me as team leader. I'd also like to find out about your career ambitions and how I could possibly be of assistance

NAME OF PERSON:

Levels of Trust	Examples	Desire for Our Relationship in the Future	What Do I Appreciate About Them?
Level 1: Able			
Level 2: Timely			

Level 3: Honest	Level 4: "For me"

PREPARATION FOR A TRUST CONVERSATION

Before bringing the worksheet to the other person for a conversation around trust and closure, reflect on the following questions:

- What would be a good environment in which to have this conversation? Reflect on the context (e.g., beginning or ending of a busy period in work/life) and the physical space that's most conducive for this conversation.
- What might this other person really want and need?
- How, as a leader, do you need to be present to them in this conversation?
- What hopes about the future relationship and thoughts about the past will you need to relinquish to be nonattached to the outcome of this meeting?

This exercise works best when both people have completed the worksheet and take at least ten minutes each to go through what they've written about the other person. Of most importance when we're listening is that we sit with each item of positive-appreciation feedback for about thirty seconds, letting it really sink in. This simple action can significantly impact our autonomic nervous system state and help us come away from this exercise feeling safe, connected, and optimistic about the development of this relationship into the future.

Chapter 10

OUR EVOLVING
LEADERSHIP

May your choices reflect your hopes, not your fears.
—Nelson Mandela

Having reflected on My Inner World in depth and begun to consider how to lead from a place of contemplation in My Outer World, this final chapter provides some signposts to how our leadership might develop into The Whole World. It introduces us to a meta model that straddles all Three Domes of Meaning and will, I hope, provide us with some inspiration for how our collective, interconnected leadership might evolve.

SPIRAL DYNAMICS

At the end of each college semester, students would ask Dr. Clare Graves which of the developmental psychology models he had taught them were "right."[1] It was 1951, and he was teaching psychology at Union College in Schenectady, New York.[2] As a specialist in the theory of personality, Graves would teach classes on all the major theorists up to that point: from Sigmund Freud and his theory of the id (our instincts and wants that unconsciously drive our behavior), ego (the logical part of us that makes realistic plans), and superego (the idealized rules-based moral code that we inherit from family and society) to Watson and Skinner and their theory of behaviorism with its contingency management (the "carrot and stick" method of motivation) and the "black box" approach to the mind (that the mind is too complex to understand because we can only see the inputs it receives and the outputs it produces). Graves would teach about the humanistic approach of Carl Rogers, with its active listening ("I feel your pain") and nondirective approach to counseling and then teach the work of his good friend, the humanistic psychologist Abraham Maslow: that individual humans are basically good, and it's just oppressive environments that adversely affect us. He would then finish his courses by teaching about the theories of cognitive sciences that were beginning to appear. But the question remained from his students: Which theory was "right"? He couldn't give them an answer because he didn't believe *any* of the approaches were "right." So, he decided to conduct his own psychological research.

Over the course of nine years, he asked thousands of respondents to complete sentences beginning with "Healthy people are . . ." and "People who have it together are . . ." and "People who understand the world are like . . . ." The results of his research differed from every model or theory he had ever taught. It took him several years to codify his research into a meta model that looks at what shapes us, what motivates us, how we develop across the lifespan, and, ultimately, the reasons why we care enough to lead.

During this research, Graves brought his data to his friend, Maslow.[3] Eventually, Maslow, too, agreed that the research pointed to more levels of human development beyond self-actualization, the top of Maslow's own "hierarchy of needs" model.[4] Graves's new model mapped out the worldviews and value systems that influence how individuals and groups adapt to change.

By the mid 1970s, fascinated by Graves's research, Professor Don Beck (whose dissertation had examined the psychological forces that produced the American Civil War) was keen to see how the Gravesian model could be used in conflict resolution (among other applications). He worked closely with Graves, helping him to further refine his research, subsequently renaming it "Spiral Dynamics."

One of the many applications of Spiral Dynamics is that of leadership development, helping us to consider:

- What is the context of our current leadership environment?
- Consequently, how do we bring the most relevant aspects of our Whole Selves to bear in ways that are most helpful for the people and systems we lead and influence?

HOW OUR LEADERSHIP CHANGES

Depending on our personality and talents, the values of our community, and the broader context of our society, we each have natural preferences toward how we lead and influence. These preferences adapt in response to changing scenarios in our personal lives as well as in the broader societal context in which we find ourselves. Considering the differing settings that require our leadership helps us become aware of the conscious—and some of the unconscious—motivations that underpin the leadership behaviors we exhibit every day.

The Spiral Dynamics model is not trying to build toward any aspirational "top level" of leadership. Instead, it gives us a framework to understand the context of our environment and therefore the kinds of leadership that are appropriate for us to display in our given context. As this context changes, it's key for us to be able to firstly understand the new context we're in and then flex and change our own leadership approach to whatever is most appropriate.

As we seek to lead from a more contemplative standpoint, it's important to reflect on which of the following nine approaches to leadership we've experienced in the past and which leadership contexts and styles we most resonate with now. There are different reasons for leading at different times in our lives, and the key for us is to remain nonattached to any one approach to leadership so that we can flex our approach to the different contexts that we encounter.

1. SURVIVING

At a fundamental level, we all find ways to have our most basic needs met, from newborn babies who cry to influence the behavior of their caregivers to people who are physically injured calling out when they need help. In moments when our survival feels threatened, we experience an amygdala hijack and enter our sympathetic nervous system state. As the logical and rational thoughts of our neocortex are suspended from our consciousness, we act and react from a place of strong emotion. We unconsciously bring these reactionary behaviors into our daily experiences, where our survival instincts are often triggered when we're not facing a life-or-death scenario. We sometimes hear people say, "I don't even know what I said in that meeting—I was really upset, I couldn't think" or, "I can't believe I did that; I was just so angry."

- Think back to a time when something in your environment triggered a strong survival-instinct reaction in you. It might have been something that somebody said or did. You or your team may have unexpectedly had to face a very challenging change in your operating environment. You moved from your "normal" behavior to a totally different way of thinking, feeling, and acting.

- What about this situation can you remember (bearing in mind that it's common to block out traumatic or extreme survival experiences and have little to no memory of them)?
- What did you do in that situation?
- What effect did this have on others around you?

2. BELONGING

Once our basic survival needs are met, we seek to lead and influence so that we feel like we belong. We want to fit in with the people who are closest to us: from our family and friends to our team, organization, community, or cultural heritage. We have a sense that these are "our people." Others in the environment are somewhat similar to us in their outlook and behavior. They make us feel part of something bigger than ourselves.

However, leading by Belonging also has its downsides. Rather than focusing on our shared similarities, we can easily become overly competitive with *other* groups. It becomes the norm to adopt a dualistic worldview in which we believe we need to beat, and sometimes even destroy, the competition. Some advocates of Carl Jung's psychological theories make the distinction between jealousy and envy; while jealousy entails wanting something that others have, envy is where we want to destroy what others have because, if we can't have it, then neither can they.* A high-school or a college-class reunion is

---

* I am indebted to the Jungian analyst, Orla Crowley, for helping me understand this distinction between jealousy and envy. She writes:

When I discuss envy and jealousy from a Jungian perspective, I associate jealousy with Eros, with warmth, with fire and desire, with a longing, with fear of losing something precious, with suspicion, and feeling threatened. It's active, pushes for

(Footnote continues)

a place where we can reconnect with old friends. Yet it is also a place where both jealousy and envy can appear. We're jealous that someone has made good money or has remained married to their childhood sweetheart; we're both happy for them and jealous of them, wishing we had something similar. Then, as we notice the group of people we never liked back in school and we get wind of their career and relational success, we might feel envious, secretly wishing that things would fall apart for them. If our envy is sufficiently strong, we might even behave in ways to damage or destroy what these other people have. If we can't have it, then neither can they.

Leading by Belonging is all about enhancing social cohesion. Adhering to certain practices and rituals facilitates this cohesion to take place—for example, when the group eats a meal together, we all sit in our usual seat; we tell the same insider jokes and revisit the handful of stories that speak to our common bonds of belonging. We share "war stories" of the challenges that hampered us for a time but that we eventually overcame together. On some level, we believe we're "better" because we're different from other groups. This kind of belonging is powerful for a time, inspiring group conformity. It brings a sense of safety, especially when the external environment is perceived

---

connection, etymologically related to zeal and zealots. It tends to exist in a three-person dynamic. "I want something of what that person has for myself."

I associate envy with Thanatos, the death instinct, coldness, a sense of inner emptiness, the painful feeling of wanting what someone else has; linked to early narcissism, a sense of inferiority, primal emotions—and an urge to destroy.

Etymologically, invidia—non-sight, blindness—perhaps a blindness to what one has oneself; also invidere—to look at with malice. It tends to be a two-person dynamic, such as in sibling rivalry. "I want to destroy what that person has because I lack precisely that."

So, highly simplistically, jealousy in this incarnation may motivate, may move to copy, to imitate; envy moves to destroy what the other has, to pull them down, to vitiate, being unable to bear the "excellence" of others.

The development of a mature, adequately functioning ego is a protection from both.

as threatening. Leaders emerge by telling stories, reminding us of our common narratives and our shared bonds. At its best, the Belonging style is healthy and stable and doesn't feel the need to destroy other groups—just as long as they don't try to interfere with us.

- Reflect on your experiences of belonging: e.g., cheering on your favorite sports team, plotting a prank with friends, or pushing to win a bid with your team at work. How do you tend to behave in these situations?
- Are you a ringleader, a loyal follower, or a tradition keeper?
- What kind of leadership behaviors tend to most influence your groups' thinking and behaviors?

3. OVERCOMING

As our external environment changes, the stability of our group becomes unbalanced, and we now need to influence in different ways. Individual leaders arise, often displaying a great sense of self-belief, a heroic vision of their own ability, and a charisma that inspires others with confidence. We build followership by displaying our prowess (our business acumen, our personal wealth, even our sexual encounters) and are great at narrating compelling stories to:

- highlight the dangers of the differences of other groups and
- outline how only *we* have the resources to overcome these dangers and lead our group to victory or safety.

When we lead in this Overcoming way, there's often a sense of confidence, a certain panache or bravado when we enter a room. Our very presence causes a reaction of some sort, a stir that puts some on edge or a thrill that makes others excited and ready for action. The focus is on our unique ability to overcome great trials and a promise that we'll bring others through great trials and adversity to restore the status quo. In exchange, we expect—even demand—unwavering loyalty from our followers.

Depictions of this form of heroic leadership are common in popular culture, from the famous freedom speech in the *Braveheart* movie and the storylines of the Marvel Cinematic Universe to books about coaches and athletes who lead their teams to victory against all odds. Popular culture goes through phases of admiring superstar CEOs with big salaries and even bigger egos who are praised for their uncanny ability to turn around jaded corporations or create entirely new organizations with hockey-stick growth curves.

At our best, as Overcoming leaders we use our huge presence to connect with large groups of people and lead them through considerable adversity. At our worst, we spend our energies building our public profile while scapegoating minorities and spreading fear among our followers.

- When have you experienced this form of leadership from others? Common examples include "clutch" moments in sports, politics, or corporate life.
- In what settings have you taken on the behaviors of an Overcoming leader? What did that feel like? How did it work out for you?

4. ESTABLISHING

The next evolution to our leadership occurs when a group of leaders establishes fundamental principles for how a growing organization is to be run. Agreeing to this set of rules prevents any one leader from taking the reins and using the organization as a personal fiefdom. Nations turn to legal codes that establish the constitutional authority of their government. Religious organizations turn to a sacred text for guidance and direction. Businesses turn to an established code of ethics, a vision, a mission, a values document, a policy paper, or a company constitution. Organizations and the wider society grow when they consistently abide by a rules-based order. A police force and the judiciary, as well as the institutions of elected government, enforce and protect the citizens under the rule of law. In each of these groups, there is a widely recognized and accepted way of doing things.

As these hierarchical and bureaucratical institutions grow, Establishing leaders at the top have the most power. We occupy roles as directors, politicians, popes, imams, monarchs, hospital directors, and school principals. Due to our roles, we become figureheads that represent the power of the overall institution.

Our role as Establishing leaders is not based on the force of our personality but on our ability to predictably and consistently steer the organization in line with its founding vision.

- What institutions have you been a part of across your life? These may include religious, political, community, national, sporting, or corporate institutions.
- What roles do you tend to take on within these various institutions?

5. OPTIMIZING

In the next iteration of leadership, the most valued leaders are those who deliver clear outcomes in the most efficient manner possible. To influence well within an Optimizing culture, we learn to quickly adapt to ever-changing scenarios and still deliver consistently great results. We learn how to take sprawling organizations and streamline them into higher levels of productivity. Or else we create something from scratch, setting strategic goals and tactical practices that teams of managers can easily enact. Iteration and innovation are part of daily life.

Our performance stands out as being better than that of others, and, consequently, we rise to the top and develop followers who want to emulate us. When leading in this way, we often value quantitative more than qualitative data because the Optimizing worldview draws deeply from scientific methodologies. Consequently, an underlying belief within this value system is that efficiencies can be found by separating out complex issues into their composite parts so we can discover, and then replace, the weakest links within our organization. This Optimizing organization should run like clockwork.

The focus here becomes very utilitarian: "If it leads to better results, we'll do it." As a result, efficient Optimizing organizations can make people feel disconnected from each other due to the transactional-style nature of interactions.

Not only does this describe the *modus operandi* of social media influencers, it also encapsulates the culture of entrepreneurship and privately owned organizations within most Western societies today. Many businesses operate within this paradigm, as it uncovers strategies to direct the behavior of internal stakeholders and control as much of the external environment as possible. It has become so prevalent, in fact, that this way of leading and influencing is considered "normal" by many. From tech companies to entire countries (like my own, which for two decades has been referred to by government ministers as "Ireland Inc."), many contemporary systems embody this worldview and seek leadership that encourages complex systems to integrate using scientific principles so they can grow along the lines of free-market economics.

If this is our baseline for what we believe good leadership is about, we look at Establishing, Overcoming, Belonging, and Surviving leadership with a degree of disdain or a sense of superiority. Perhaps our parents or grandparents operated that way then, or maybe we did, too, when we were younger. But now we know better than that. And while we may look back with a degree of smugness, we also look out at other approaches we have not yet experienced (such as the next one, Including) with a degree of skepticism. We believe they're too different, too left or right of center, and that our Optimizing approach is the best, as it delivers results.

- From your own experience, what organizations most epitomize this Optimizing approach to leadership?
- How do you tend to behave within this kind of a paradigm? For example, do you buy into it wholeheartedly and push for great results, or do you have a different approach entirely?
- What would be possible for you to achieve if you were to approach leadership a little more in this Optimizing way?

6. INCLUDING

A time comes in the life of many leaders when they are compelled to influence in ways beyond mere Optimization. This next evolution in our leadership happens when we realize that there's more to any organization or movement than what's contained in the quantitative data, the metrics. Simply creating more elegant efficiencies is no longer satisfying. We've spent so long prioritizing results that we've missed out on some of the richness of human connection. Including leaders, instead, create cultures that focus on finding ways for people to relate to and understand each other.

We create the conditions and the space to hear everyone's story because we believe that stories have the power to connect people and invite individuals into community. We influence by facilitating inclusive social interactions within our organization and wider society.

We focus on personalizing the efficient systems that have emerged, and we promote social cohesion by emphasizing the inclusion of all voices and narratives. Organizational programs around well-being and concepts such as "purpose and profit" help us straddle the threshold between leading by Optimizing and leading by Including.

- Have you ever experienced this Including approach to leadership?
- If so, what effect did it have on you?
- In what current scenarios could you facilitate the conditions for different narratives to be told and divergent perspectives to be heard?

This is the beginning of a contemplative approach to leadership, where not only are we nonattached to seeing and doing things our way—we're also now actively pursuing seeing things the way others see them. As this develops into Adapting, we are actively trying to find ways of doing things that work best for others *and* benefit ourselves. The zero-sum game is being deconstructed, and we're seeking to develop win-win relationships and business scenarios.

As we become aware of the breadth and depth of our current context, we can move from fear to curiosity, from control to openness, from isolation to connection with others. This enables us to make decisions and act even when we don't have all the data points at our disposal.

To get to this place of being comfortable with uncertainty requires far more than a simple "aha" moment or a mindset shift. It involves a holistic exploration of what has shaped us and a radical acceptance of who we are. In going to the depths of ourselves, of how and why we lead, we gain a better grasp of our limitations and set healthy boundaries within which we can influence in powerful ways.

7. ADAPTING

Having been influenced by Including for a period of time, listening to the stories of all stakeholders, understanding different narratives, and seeking to navigate paradoxical and often competing perspectives, some leaders then go through a significant internal metamorphosis. We no longer look back with disdain at some of our earlier manifestations of leadership. Instead, we realize that there's a time and a place to create a sense of Belonging by defining ourselves by who we are not; to lead by Overcoming great obstacles; to bring stability by honoring the traditions of our organization, religion, or society by adhering to Established rules and practices; to Optimize and find efficiencies in how we work together and deliver results; to Include the voices of all individuals and groups. We recognize that, based on our lived experiences, we can adapt to the scenarios we face by prioritizing how best to influence within each of life's unique circumstances.

This development of an Adapting approach to leadership is, according to Spiral Dynamics, the first of a new, "second tier" of conscious awareness that humans can develop.[5] As Adapting leaders, we come to see our primary leadership responsibility as adapting to the needs and the motivations of the various individuals, groups, and communities that we lead. When a global pandemic or a business crisis occurs, we connect with our own Survival needs and are therefore able to hear and understand the needs of others whose behaviors are being driven by a fundamental drive to keep their jobs, their homes, and their health. When there is a new pollutant threat to our local environment, we instill a sense of togetherness within the community, inspiring everyone to act toward a common cause. We identify the charismatic Overcomers within our team and empower them to take some risks in how they expand the market share of the business. We listen to the Establishing rule keepers who want to maintain balance and appropriate accountability on expenditure within the city council. We empower the Optimizers to find efficiencies, to change tactics, and reform aspects of the system that need an overhaul. We facilitate and advocate for the Includers to get broad buy-in from a wide constituency of diverse voices across the organization. We adapt our style and approach wherever appropriate, seeing the importance of everyone and encouraging others to take responsibility for the areas of the organization that are most important to them.

Adapting leaders are humble and motivated more by the common good than by our own egoistic need to succeed or be proven right. We are confident enough within ourselves that we can delegate, coach, listen to, and guide others. But we can also be directive and forthright in our leadership style and communication tone. It all depends on the situation. As Adapting leaders, we spend our time empowering *others* to take responsibility and lead in ways that are both natural to them and beneficial for the whole organization. We become more comfortable with paradox, with not knowing things with certainty, and with being part of a seemingly chaotic system that grows more like an ecosystem than like a tightly wound mechanism.

The nonattachment of Adapting leadership is what gives us the presence to influence others and the system in a seemingly hands-off way. But this nonattachment does not mean that we are in any way disengaged. Quite the opposite, in fact; nonattachment allows us, as Adapting leaders, to be fully engaged without overidentifying with just one or two approaches to each leadership scenario we face. We can both focus on the specific details of our daily decisions and communication and maintain a broader perspective on the macro environment that impacts everything we do. We connect the dots between the wider world and our daily realities and call on the greatest abilities of those we lead and influence to contribute in ways that are most natural to them.

As we hone our abilities to lead different people in different ways, we begin to see more of the interconnections between public and private, personal and community, national and global. We experience the deeply woven connections between our cognition, emotions, and physiology and between all people, ecosystems, and species that live and die together on our planet. Over time, as Adapting leaders we begin to find like-minded people who share similar perspectives on leadership that are based on their *own* lived experiences. As we come together with these groups of leaders, often from very different backgrounds, we integrate our knowledge and wisdom in deeply interconnected ways.

- Reflect on a time when you changed your approach to influencing someone based on their needs: e.g., speaking to a child, a junior work colleague, a manager, a very intellectual person, an empathetic colleague, an achievement-oriented friend. How easy was it for you to adapt your approach?
- How do you balance being authentic with adapting your approach to communicate well and connect with others?

8. INTERCONNECTING

Over time, Adapting leaders gravitate toward each other and form groups and communities of Interconnecting leaders. Often not working together in the same organization, as Interconnecting leaders we bring together our varied backgrounds and uncover surprising synergies. Our relationships and conversations are part of the ever-unfolding interconnecting of culture, market forces, team dynamics, and individual contribution. To use the German word *gestalt*, we are now leading in ways that value the whole picture as being greater than the sum of its parts. For example, we take the experience of building a business—understanding the economic and business cycles, customer needs, team dynamics, and organizational structures—and learn from other Interconnecting leaders about how we can embrace their expertise as well. To uncover the patterns that exist in our seemingly chaotic world, we might integrate what we already know with elements of artificial intelligence, seeking to simplify aspects of our systems and create opportunities for new perspectives or new clients to emerge. We move away from oversimplistic, reductionistic perspectives of "good or bad," of "right or wrong," of being "attached or detached," and instead learn to think in non-dualistic ways. As we spend time with other Interconnecting leaders, we embrace embodied practices together that include our mind, body, and soul connections, from yoga to contemplative sits to cold water immersion. This allows us to experience embodied systems interconnectivity in a way that the rational, dualistic mind is just too limited to see.

We learn to embrace daily life experiences and see leadership opportunities in a nonattached, contemplative way. We can step in to complex and seemingly chaotic scenarios and resist the temptation to control them. We can see how, similar to in an ecosystem, some systems connect well together, others don't integrate, and some live off the detritus of other systems. Interconnecting is not always an efficient way of developing or of leading, but it mirrors the evolutionary processes that have led to us being alive today.

As we become more comfortable with paradox, not always needing definitive answers to our questions, we create the conditions for ideas and systems to organically emerge over time. We experientially learn that even tiny changes to our leadership can have huge effects on our wider spheres of influence. This happens whether we are aware of the principles of quantum mechanics and chaos theory, which teach us about the interconnectivity of all matter and the patterns that exist amongst seemingly "chaotic" systems. Interconnecting leaders participate in and sometimes birth ecosystems that are constantly growing in new directions.

My experience of Interconnecting leaders is that, energetically, they don't come across as being quite as driven as they used to be when they were much younger. They seem much more in a flow state whereby they lean in and apply their considerable skills and work ethic in service to the collective. But they also know how to step back, pause to ponder, discuss their initiatives, and reflect on their emerging hypotheses. This ability to modulate between intense work and deep inactivity is an acquired practice that sets these Interconnecting leaders apart.

This interconnected way of thinking and experiencing reality is quite rare, and these leaders really appreciate a place of community, encouragement, and depth of relationship with other Interconnecting leaders.

- What is your experience of integrating different, seemingly unrelated systems into your leadership (for instance, mixing human psychology with cultural anthropology to lead an international team at work)?
- What's your experience of *both* working very hard *and* also taking time to ponder? How do you feel on an emotional level when you stop your activity and take time to reflect on what you're doing (e.g., you might feel very comfortable pausing, guilty that you're not "working," or something else)?
- What Interconnecting leaders can you learn from?

9. EVOLVING

Not a lot is known about what this next evolution in leadership and consciousness is all about. But as the biosphere of our planet evolves, as market forces of commerce and political systems inevitably change, as they have done for millennia, the combination of evolving technology and human development will further resemble ecosystems that are governed by principles of evolution more than by the structures of human hierarchies that can be neatly controlled. To lead in this way involves us going on an internal journey of evolution and continuing on this path for the duration of our life.

Embracing internal change requires an attitude of self-compassion and a playful curiosity toward ourselves and the world around us. Change here is seen as natural and good, where we are neither overly attached to maintaining the status quo nor running away from our commitments and responsibilities toward the latest technology or newest systems adaptation. We embrace the flow of evolutionary emergence, with lots of micro experiments and iterations along the way. We move three steps forward and two steps back, and sometimes two steps forward and three steps back. Our failures are seen as just another part of how we grow. As we change within, we continue to bring that change to everyone and every situation without.

Presence, perspective, embracing paradox with a contemplative mind (and yet choosing to act with courage and empathy for the collective needs of the environment), technology, and all sentient beings are of most importance as leaders evolve.

- Tracing your own leadership influence, how have periods of significant internal growth affected change for the people and organizations around you?
- Recall a time when you were unnecessarily resistant to change (e.g., in a conflict scenario with someone or when you oversaw others' work.) How did this experience affect your own growth as a leader? How did this experience, and your own growth, impact others?
- Read over the last two paragaphs one more time and then write a few sentences on your future vision for yourself as an Evolving leader.

CONCLUSION

We all modulate between several of these approaches to leadership during any one phase in our life. Of most importance is that we notice what is most natural to us at *this* moment in time and ask ourselves which approach is best suited to the value systems we encounter in our organizations, our communities, and our relationships—personal as well as professional. Developmentally, we all start off as children learning to Survive on a basic level, Belong with our peers, Overcome challenges, and Establish ourselves within society—and some of us go even further, into Optimizing our efforts, Including others, and beyond. No single approach is better than any other; there's a time and a place for each approach to leadership. What approach to use and when will depend on our awareness of what's most important to us at this point in our lives and the values that most underpin our current leadership context.

To further develop as a leader across all Three Domes of Meaning, we need to reexamine the reasons why we used to lead in the past. In today's Western cultures, where the focus is usually on Optimizing and a little on Including, that means we need to revisit how we act when situations require us to engage our Survival, Belonging, Overcoming, or Establishing leadership. This counterintuitive approach to growing within an Optimizing or Including system allows us to dig deeper and strengthen the very roots of our leadership presence.

As we become more self-aware and more practiced at leading in these different ways, we may notice ourselves being drawn towards Adapting ways of leading and beyond. The focus, however, is not to keep growing and evolving; it's far more important that we become aware of our own leadership values and can answer the questions of:

- Why do I lead?
- And, therefore, what am I trying to build as a result?

Fundamentally, we're then able to honestly assess if our approach is broadly aligned with the values and drivers of the organizational systems in which we lead.

And once we have some degree of clarity on the answers to these two questions, we then return to the fundamental questions of:

- How can I lead in this context from a place of nonattachment, from a place of contemplation?
- What would be the subtle and not-so-subtle characteristics of my leadership if I were to be present but not controlling in how I influence others?

CODA

Integration Exercise

We have covered many different themes and examined several interconnected frameworks across parts one and two of the book. Although the diagrams have sought to aid our understanding of how seemingly disparate elements are related (between our Inner and Outer Worlds, our conscious and unconscious awareness, our False Self and our True Self), the following exercise can help us further integrate the lessons from the exercises in each chapter.

INTEGRATION EXERCISE

Review your exercise notes from previous chapters, especially what you wrote on the blank Three Domes of Meaning diagram on page 158. Populate each dome with your answers and notice the patterns and overlaps that emerge across each of the domes:

IDENTITIES

- How does what you wrote link with your identities?
- Which identities seem quite intrinsic, very much a part of your Inner World?
- Which identities seem to have developed more extrinsically to meet the requirements of group belonging and group identity in your Outer World?
- Which identities most connect your Inner and Outer Worlds with The Whole World?

VALUES

- What do you most value in your Inner World?
- What do you most value in your Outer World, in your interactions with the communities and groups where you lead others and where others influence you?
- What do you value about The Whole World?

CHALLENGE AND FAILURE

- How have challenges and failures from across the Three Domes impacted you?
- For example, from The Whole World, what illnesses or bereavements, accidents or natural disasters have reshaped how you view your place in the cosmos?
- From your Outer World, what challenging relationships and group interactions have impacted your leadership presence and capacity to influence others?
- From within your Inner World, when has your narrative of success, your "script," been challenged by personal disappointments such as:
  - not achieving certain results?
  - not performing well as a leader?
  - not living up to your inner values?

- ○ not being courageous in your pursuit of your personal best?

THE HERO'S JOURNEY

Within the context of the Hero's Journey, are you:

- Being invited to Depart your Ordinary World and Descend into a new phase of exploration and discovery?
- In the midst of a Descent, a season of life where old ways of being and perceiving are being stripped away?
- Moving from Descent toward a Return to the Ordinary World, with a deeper sense of what's meaningful to you and what is yours to contribute in how you lead in your Ordinary World?

POLYVAGAL STATES

Reflecting on your ventral vagal nervous system state:

- Which aspects from each of these Three Domes of Meaning make you feel connected, safe, and regulated? For example, living out your personal values from within your Inner World can make you feel content and connected. Spending time with certain groups and individuals from your Outer World can help you co-regulate and feel calm and comfortable. Living within an overarching meta-narrative from your religion or your philosophy as part of your understanding of The Whole World can give you a sense of acceptance, hope, and meaning.
- Which elements from across all three domes make you feel dysregulated, vigilant, unsafe in some ways, or just "not yourself"? Become aware of your gut instinct, your intuition, and write down a few unfiltered thoughts.

CONTEMPLATION

Paying attention to what stands out to you as emerging themes across all Three Domes of Meaning, what are you now more aware of than you were before? What do you need to be more present to in your life now? For example, are there relationships that you have been taking for granted, important people that you have not been paying attention to in the ways you really want? Are you now seeing the importance of a meta-narrative, an overarching raison d'être, for the first time? Or are you simply being reminded that you've been on autopilot for a long time, and now you want to explore the fundamental purpose of your life, your leadership, and your legacy to gain more clarity on what's important to you *now*? Perhaps you're realizing that you've been mainly driven by external forces—from organizational culture, parental or spousal expectations, a reaction against your poor upbringing that drove you to "succeed" materially and in your career—and that now is the time to move away from "reacting" against past experiences as a way of making life choices. Instead, you get to go a layer deeper and "respond" from inside your Inner World.

Take some time to listen to yourself, to explore what's most fundamental about you, what gives you the deepest sense of meaning, and, therefore, what the internal source of your leadership and influence is in the world.

OUR EVOLVING LEADERSHIP

Look over the nine approaches to evolving leadership outlined in the last chapter and notice which approach you predominantly operate from now. Then reflect on the following:

- Which of these approaches is your most natural, personal preference of leadership (My Inner World)?

- Which approach most matches the needs of the people you currently lead in your organization/community/society (My Outer World)?
- Considering The Whole World narrative that frames your overarching worldview, which approach to leadership best corresponds to how you would *ideally* like to lead?

Tension will exist within us if there is a huge difference between our *ideal* approach and our current approach to leadership. This is where a contemplative approach to leadership is helpful, where self-awareness identifies a difference between what we would like and what we currently have. If this describes your current leadership scenario, then answer the following questions:

- Which of your values do you need to most focus on right now? These will keep you grounded and present to the current challenges you're facing.
- Within which of the Three Domes of Meaning do you need to focus most of your attention? Focusing here will help you restore a sense of connection to what is most meaningful to you today.
- What about your current scenario is both challenging yet important to accept? There will be a sense of loss and personal suffering involved in fully accepting your current reality.
- What ideas and hopes do you need to let go of for now? This will require you to move from being attached to being nonattached to good, worthwhile narratives and initiatives. However, this will also allow you to become more present to the day-to-day realities of your leadership context.

APPENDIX

Origins of Contemplative Practices in the West

T here's nothing new about contemplation as a practice and a perspective on life. It is a way of perceiving reality and experiencing each moment that has been around for thousands of years, across many religious and philosophical traditions. It has experienced a resurgence in the West for close to a century now, drawing on Buddhist and other Eastern, as well as Jewish and Christian, traditions.

Inspired by a Jewish practice of leaving society for a time to live in the desert, the Desert Mothers and Fathers left the city of Alexandria and lived in small communities or as hermits in the Egyptian desert from the fourth century onwards. These generations, who spent much of their time in silence and solitude, developed a whole other tradition of meditative practices, which subsequently became known as "contemplative practices."[1] These practices formed the basis of Celtic Christianity and other monastic communities and movements that emerged throughout Europe over the centuries that followed.

Due to the Greek philosophical traditions in the West that emphasized rational thinking, by the twelfth century the word "meditation" had come to mean a form of reflection on a thought or a concept.[2] So it was at this point that the term "contemplative practices" came into usage to describe the noncognitive practices that Eastern traditions referred to as "meditation."

Monasticism that stressed these contemplative practices slowly gave way to scholasticism from the mid to late Medieval period up until the beginning of the Reformation (c. 1100–1517 CE). Scholasticism was a system of theology and philosophy taught in medieval European universities that emphasized Aristotelian logic and a spirituality that focused on tradition and dogma. Then, from the Reformation onward, contemplative traditions were sidelined even further as the Western world focused more on the rational thinking of the Enlightenment (e.g., "I think, therefore I am," of René Descartes[3]), which in turn led to the mechanistic thinking that gave birth to the Industrial Revolution (inputs, throughputs, and outputs). The scientific method of deduction, of testing a hypothesis through experimentation, emerged as the normal way of learning about life. Isaac Newton stated his third law of motion: "For every action there is an equal and opposite reaction." In such a context, contemplative practices and contemplative ways of seeing and experiencing life seemed old-fashioned and irrelevant. And as history ran its course, right up to the early twentieth century, these dominant approaches to knowledge and to life that most valued rational, logical, evidence-based thinking led to the era known as Modernism.

There was a general belief that the applications of the scientific method could lead to the resolution of many of the world's challenges, from healthcare provision (e.g., more and more disease vaccinations and cures) to world peace (e.g., ending conflicts more effectively). Then World War I took place, with millions of casualties, shocking the psyche of Western European countries in particular. A global economic crisis followed the 1929 Wall Street crash, bringing abject poverty to many millions around the world. And then World War II happened, putting a final nail in the coffin of the sincere hopes of Modernism.

Around this time, Thomas Merton decided to become a monk in the Abbey of Gethsemani, Kentucky. Over his years of solitude, reading, and writing, he reintroduced contemplative ways of experiencing reality to his readers in the United States and around the world. His deep interest in contemplation led to an interfaith dialogue with Buddhist teachers, including the Dalai Lama in 1968. During this same period, the English-born Alan Watts published his first book about Zen Buddhism in the 1930s. Beginning with *The Spirit of Zen*, he wrote many other books, including *The Way of Zen* and *Behold the Spirit: A Study in the Necessity of Mystical Religion*. His work sought to bring the practical applications of various Eastern philosophies and religions, including meditation, into mainstream Western awareness.

Contemplative practices and communities of meditation continued to develop in the West (e.g., through Thomas Keating, John Main, Laurence Freeman, and Richard Rohr) while at the same time, from the 1980s onwards, very similar though subtly different Buddhist meditative practices began to be integrated into Western medical settings by Jon Kabat-Zinn, an emeritus professor of medicine at the University of Massachusetts Medical School. He had been influenced by Buddhist teachers such as Philip Kapleau, Seungsahn, and a leading advocate of "engaged Buddhism" in the West, the Vietnamese Thiền Buddhist monk, Thích Nhất Hạnh. But Kabat-Zinn moved away from a Buddhist framing of meditation and focused on a scientific basis for his program. His research and the ensuing courses provided very positive outcomes that helped course participants to cope with stress and pain and even illness by focusing on "moment-to-moment awareness."[4] Kabat-Zinn's adaptation of Eastern meditative practices came to be known as Mindfulness, which he defined as "Paying attention on purpose, in the present moment, and nonjudgmentally."[5] Over the last few decades, similar work was developed in the United Kingdom by, among others, Mark Williams, an emeritus professor of psychology at Oxford University. His research built on Kabat-Zinn's Mindfulness-Based Stress Reduction (MBSR) program and led to the creation of Mindfulness-Based Cognitive Therapy (MBCT).[6] The focus of Kabat-Zinn and Williams on a contemplative, "inside out" approach to meditation has been researched for many decades now, with a substantial body of evidence pointing to meditation practitioners having lower stress levels, a higher sense of well-being, higher job satisfaction, more effective decision-making, higher levels of workplace engagement, fewer thoughts of leaving their jobs, and a higher level of job performance.[7]

The ancient, traditional practices that once seemed esoteric or outdated to contemporary healthcare workers are now forming part of mainstream treatment and prevention of all sorts of stress-related illnesses. Mindfulness has been rigorously researched in academic circles, with studies pointing to Mindfulness practitioners being able to tune out distractions, improve their memory and attention, and experience boosts to their immune systems.[8] Measurements of neuroplasticity, changes in the structure of the human brain, find that Mindfulness practitioners experience a densification of brain cells in regions linked to emotional regulation, empathy, learning, and memory.[9] Mindfulness meditation CDs grew in popularity, and now Mindfulness apps have gone viral, with millions of people around the world beginning to engage in secular meditative practices for the first time. Today, there is a significant body of medical and other Western academic research pointing to the profound benefits of the contemplative practice of meditation.

ACKNOWLEDGMENTS

Firstly, I'd like to thank my wife, Jess, for her unwavering love and support. It's been inspiring to see you embrace your own leadership presence and influence over the last few years. We've certainly weathered some storms throughout this latest season of writing! I'm so glad we faced them together.

To Scott Hill, whose conversations around contemplation and leadership crystallized my thoughts on using "nonattached" as a synonym for "contemplation." Thanks for all the great chats we've had over the last twenty-plus years. You truly are a font of wisdom and a great friend.

Sincere thanks to Paul Higgins, the person who asks more questions than anyone else I know! I've greatly appreciated your excitement and belief in my work as we discussed the content of this book over many sailing trips.

To Sr. Peggy at the Glendalough Hermitage in Wicklow, thank you for taking such good care of me during my visits, for curating your wonderful library, and for leaving those books on my doorstep first thing in the morning.

To Orla Crowley, whose insights into Jungian analysis have been profoundly helpful to me in every way. Thank you for your great assistance in tracing the distinctions between "jealousy" and "envy."

To Katie Dickman, thank you for your abundance of kindness, your calm, and your clarity throughout each step of the writing process. It's been a joy to work with you.

I'd like to thank Jim McNeish for your generosity over the years and for giving me permission to adapt your wonderful model on "trust."

To Rachel Delap, for all the subtlety, understatement, and beauty you bring to each of your designs—thank you. You make it so enjoyable and effortless to work with you.

To Matthew McCarthy, who took such time and interest in walking through each edit of our interview together. Your considered reflections, passion for an equitable world, and deep commitment to those you lead set you apart as a leader worth following.

Thanks to Ben Keesey for your unquestioning support and commitment to this project. You've been teaching me about contemplative leadership since the first day we met.

To Louise Chester—your enthusiasm for this book has buoyed me along from the first moment I mentioned it to you. Thanks for giving so generously of your time for our interview. Your insights and grounded presence continue to inspire everyone you encounter.

To Meg Wheatley, a leader of unparalleled vision and energy. After all the years of reading your work, I remember the sense of amazement in bumping into you that time in Ghost Ranch. "Synchronicity," we called it. I feel very privileged to have had you reflect on your life and career with me during our interview for this book.

To Richard Rohr, the embodiment of a contemplative who never thinks of himself as a leader! A friend, mentor, and "third grandfather" to my son, your trust continues to be a priceless gift. I loved when, during our interview, you came up with the three perspectives of "glaring, glancing, and gazing." Thank you for your foreword, your friendship, and for continually sharing your deep wisdom with us all.

To my son, Patrick. Your deep curiosity, sense of humour, kind heart, and grounded presence reminds me of what's most important in life. I love you and enjoy every moment of being your dad.

NOTES

INTRODUCTION

1 From "Burnt Norton," from *Four Quartets* by T. S. Eliot. Copyright © 1936 by Houghton Mifflin Harcourt Publishing Company, renewed 1964 by T.S. Eliot. Copyright © 1940, 1941, 1942 by T.S. Eliot, renewed 1968, 1969, 1970 by Esme Valerie Eliot. Used by permission of HarperCollins Publishers. Eliot, T S. 2019. *Four Quartets*. S.L.: Faber And Faber.

2 Manchán Magan, "Breaking Bread," July 14, 2021, in *The Almanac of Ireland*, produced by RTÉ, podcast, 17:00, https://www.rte.ie/radio/podcasts/21980661-breaking-bread/.

3 Jennifer Mackewn, "Understanding the Paradoxical Theory of Change," in *Developing Gestalt Counselling: A Field Theoretical and Relational Model of Contemporary Gestalt Counselling and Psychotherapy* (London: SAGE Publications, 1997).

4 Thomas Merton, *New Seeds of Contemplation* (Boulder, CO: Shambhala, 2003), 36–37. Merton's descriptions of the terms *True Self* and *False Self* have become a foundational piece of contemporary spirituality and have clarified for many that we must let go of the False Self so that the True Self, the most authentic part of us, can come to the fore.

5 Ibid.

6 Model adapted from Robert Dilts and Robert McDonald, *Tools of the Spirit* (Capitola, CA: Meta Publications, 1997), 35.

7 Model adapted with permission from Richard Rohr, *Things Hidden: Scripture as Spirituality* (Cincinnati, OH: Franciscan Media, 2022), 17.

CHAPTER 1

1 Richard Rohr, "Becoming a Grand Parent," Center for Action and Contemplation, September 23, 2022, https://cac.org/daily-meditations/becoming-a-grand-parent-2022-09-23/.

2 George Fink, *Stress Science: Neuroendocrinology* (Elsevier Science, 2009): 401; Martin Corbett, "From Law to Folklore: Work Stress and the Yerkes-Dodson Law," *Journal of Managerial Psychology* 30, no. 6 (2015): 741–52, doi:10.1108/JMP-03-2013-0085.

3 Samuel Beckett, "The Unnamable," in *Three Novels: Molloy, Malone Dies, The Unnamable* (New York: Grove Press, 2009).

4 According to Mihaly Csikszentmihalyi, we have the capacity to consciously process up to 126 bits of data per second. See Mihaly Csikszentmihalyi, *Flow: The Psychology of Optimal Experience* (New York: HarperCollins, 1990), 29. With far more data than that available to us each second, our brain's "attentional filter" of neurons assesses which data is most important and directs us where to focus our moment-by-moment attention. See Daniel J. Levitin, *The Organized Mind: Thinking Straight in the Age of Information Overload* (New York: Dutton, 2014), 17.

5 Sara W. Lazar et al., "Meditation Experience Is Associated with Increased Cortical Thickness," *NeuroReport* 16, no. 17 (2005): 1893–97, doi:10.1097/01.wnr.0000186598.66243.19.

6 Simon Grégoire, Lise Lachance, and Geneviève Taylor, "Mindfulness, Mental Health, and Emotion Regulation Among Workers," *International Journal of Wellbeing* 5, no. 4 (2015): 96–119, doi:10.5502/ijw.v5i4.444; Mark Craigie et al., "A Pilot Evaluation of a Mindful Self-Care and Resiliency (MSCR) Intervention for Nurses," *Mindfulness* 7, no. 3 (2016): 764–74, doi:10.1007/s12671-016-0516-x.

7 Lazar et al., "Meditation Experience Is Associated with Increased Cortical Thickness."

8 Amishi P. Jha et al., "Examining the Protective Effects of Mindfulness Training on Working Memory Capacity and Affective Experience," *Emotion* 10, no. 1 (2010): 54–64, doi.org:10.1037/a0018438; Brigid Schulte, "Harvard Neuroscientist: Meditation Not Only Reduces Stress, Here's How It Changes Your Brain," *Washington Post*, May 26, 2015, https://www.washingtonpost.com/news/inspired-life/wp/2015/05/26/harvard-neuroscientist-meditation-not-only-reduces-stress-it-literally-changes-your-brain/.

9 Beth A. Steinberg, Maryanna Klatt, and Anne-Marie Duchemin, "Feasibility of a Mindfulness-Based Intervention for Surgical Intensive Care Unit Personnel," *American Journal of Critical Care* 26, no. 1 (2017): 10–18, doi:10.4037/ajcc2017444.

10 The text for this self-guided sit is adapted from Patrick Boland, *The Universal Christ: Companion Guide for Individuals* (CAC Publishing, 2020), 15–21.

CHAPTER 2

1 Diane K. Osbon, ed., *Reflections on the Art of Living: A Joseph Campbell Companion*, (New York: HarperCollins, 1991), 8, 24.

2 Ibid.

3 Ibid.

4 "I AM . . . With Jonny Wilkinson," July 6, 2022, in *The High Performance Podcast*, podcast, 2:08:00, https://www.thehighperformancepodcast.com /podcast/jonnywilkinson-iamcollab.

5 Ibid.

6 Ibid.

7 Richard Rohr, *Everything Belongs: The Gift of Contemplative Prayer* (New York: Crossroad Publishing Company, 2014), 142–44.

8 "I AM . . . With Jonny Wilkinson."

9 Rohr, *Everything Belongs*.

CHAPTER 3

1 About page, Stephen W. Porges, PhD, website, accessed May 26, 2023, https://www.stephenporges.com/about.

2 Deb Dana, *The Polyvagal Theory in Therapy: Engaging the Rhythm of Regulation* (New York: W. W. Norton & Company, 2018), 9.

3 Daniel Goleman, *Emotional Intelligence: Why It Can Matter More than IQ* (London: Bloomsbury, 1995).

4 Jeffrey K. Aronson, "'Where Name and Image Meet'—the Argument for 'Adrenaline,'" *BMJ* 320 (2000): 506–9, doi:10.1136/bmj.320.7233.506.

5 "Hunter-Gatherer Culture," National Geographic, accessed May 26, 2023, https://education.nationalgeographic.org/resource/hunter-gatherer-culture/.

6 Gina Ryder, "The Fawn Response: How Trauma Can Lead to People-Pleasing," January 10, 2022, PsychCentral, https://psychcentral.com/health /fawn-response.

7 Dana, *The Polyvagal Theory in Therapy*, 136; Deb Dana, *Polyvagal Exercises for Safety and Connection: 50 Client-Centered Practices* (New York: W. W. Norton & Company, 2018), 131, 261.

8 Nobuhiko Eda, Hironaga Ito, and Takao Akama, "Beneficial Effects of Yoga Stretching on Salivary Stress Hormones and Parasympathetic Nerve Activity," *Journal of Sports Science & Medicine* 19, no. 4 (2020): 695–702, https://www.ncbi.nlm.nih.gov/pmc/articles/PMC7675619/.

9 Dana, *The Polyvagal Theory in Therapy*, 41.

10 Ibid., 152.

11 "Psychology to Grin About: The Benefits of Smiling and Laughter," June 6, 2019, University of West Alabama, https://online.uwa.edu/news/benefits-of -smiling-and-laughter/.

12 Eda, Ito, and Akama, "Beneficial Effects of Yoga Stretching on Salivary Stress Hormones and Parasympathetic Nerve Activity."

13 "Why Does Stretching Feel Good?" August 25, 2021, Neurosurgery & Spine Consultants, https://neuroandspineconsultants.com/blog/why-does-stretching -feel-good/.

14 Adapted from Deb Dana's Personal Profile Map in Dana, *The Polyvagal Theory in Therapy*, 9, 41, 137, 152.

15 Adapted from the Ventral Vagal Anchors—Anchoring in Safety Exercise, in Dana, *Polyvagal Exercises for Safety and Connection*, 47–50, 206–207.

CHAPTER 4

1 Anthony De Mello, *Awareness: The Perils and Opportunities of Reality*, ed. J. Francis Stroud (New York: Image, 1990).

2 Jennifer A. Mangels et al., "Why do beliefs about intelligence influence learning success? A social cognitive neuroscience model," *Social Cognitive and Affective Neuroscience* 1, no. 2 (2006): 75–86, doi:10.1093/scan/nsl013.

3 Ibid.

4 Ibid.

5 Ibid.

6 Ibid.

7 Moheb Costandi, *Neuroplasticity* (Cambridge, MA: MIT Press, 2016).

8 Brené Brown, "We need to talk about shame | Brené Brown," July 31, 2021, TED, YouTube video, 1:54, https://youtu.be/5C6UELitWkw.

9 Ibid.

10 Ibid.

11 Sara W. Lazar et al., "Meditation Experience Is Associated with Increased Cortical Thickness," NeuroReport 16, no. 17 (2005): 1893–97, doi:10.1097/01.wnr.0000186598.66243.19.

12 Mei-Kei Leung et al., "Meditation-Induced Neuroplastic Changes in Amygdala Activity during Negative Affective Processing," *Social Neuroscience* 13, no. 3 (2018): 277–88, doi:10.1080/17470919.2017.1311939.

13 Viktor Frankl, *Man's Search for Meaning* (Boston: Beacon Press, 2006).

CHAPTER 5

1 K. K. Ganguly, "Life of M.K. Gandhi: A Message to Youth of Modern India," *Indian Journal of Medical Research* 149 (2019): S145–51, doi:10.4103/0971-5916.251672.

2 Gregory Bateson, *Mind and Nature: A Necessary Unity* (New York: Dutton, 1979).

3 Ibid., 92.

4   Robert Dilts, "A Brief History of Logical Levels." nlpu.com, accessed June 21, 2023, http://www.nlpu.com/Articles/LevelsSummary.htm.

5   Robert Dilts and Robert McDonald, *Tools of the Spirit* (Capitola, CA: Meta Publications, 1997), 18.

6   Ibid., 35.

7   Ibid.

CHAPTER 6

1   Margaret J. Wheatley, *Leadership and the New Science: Discovering Order in a Chaotic World* (San Francisco, CA: Berrett-Koehler Publishers, 2006).

2   "Current Thinking," Margaret J. Wheatley website, accessed April 23, 2023, https://margaretwheatley.com/library/current-thinking/.

3   "What Shambhala Is," Shambhala.org, accessed April 23, 2023, https://shambhala.org/about/what-shambhala-is/.

4   Margaret J. Wheatley, *Who Do We Choose to Be? Facing Reality, Claiming Leadership, Restoring Sanity* (San Francisco, CA: Berrett-Koehler Publishers, 2023), 293.

5   C. G. Jung, *Collected Works of C. G. Jung, Volume 8: Structure & Dynamics of the Psyche*, eds. Gerhard Adler and R. F. C. Hull (Princeton, NJ: Princeton University Press, 1970).

6   John Rowan, *Personification: Using the Dialogical Self in Psychotherapy and Counselling* (Oxfordshire, UK: Routledge, 2010).

CHAPTER 7

1   David Whyte, *Consolations: The Solace, Nourishment and Underlying Meaning of Everyday Words* (Langley, WA: Many Rivers Press, 2020), 17. Reprinted with permission from Many Rivers Press, Langley, WA, www.davidwhyte.com.

2   "Best Purpose Statement Examples from the Fortune 500," Purpose Brand, August 16, 2021, https://purposebrand.com/blog/best-purpose-statements -fortune-500/.

3   Aristotle, *Nicomachean Ethics*, trans. H. Rackham (Cambridge, MA: Harvard University Press, 1934).

4   Mark 8:36, New English Translation.

5   Viktor Frankl, *Man's Search for Meaning: An Introduction to Logotherapy* (New York: Washington Square Press, 1963), 131, 164.

6   Victor Frankl, *The Doctor and the Soul: From Psychotherapy to Logotherapy* (New York: Bantam Books, 1971).

7   "Passio," Online Etymology Dictionary, accessed March 6, 2023, https://www.etymonline.com/search?q=passio.

8   The poem "Ithaka" appears on pp. 67 & 69 (translation) in our 2009 edition, *C. P. CAVAFY: Collected Poems*, Bilingual Edition translated by Edmund

Keeley and Philip Sherrard, edited by George Savidis, with a new foreword by Robert Pinsky. English translations copyright © 1975, 1992, 2009 by Edmund Keeley and Philip Sherrard.

9   C. G. Jung, Aniela Jaffé, Clara Winston, and Richard Winston, *Memories, Dreams, Reflections* (New York: Vintage Books, 1989), 382.

10 "Cosmos, Liturgy, and the Arts in the Twelfth Century—Hildegard's Illuminated 'Scivias,'" Medieval Histories Nature History Heritage, December 28, 2022, https://www.medieval.eu/cosmos-liturgy-and-the-arts-in-the-twelfth-century-hildegards-illuminated-scivias/.

11 Adapted with permission from Richard Rohr, *Things Hidden*: Scripture and Spirituality (Cincinnati, OH: Franciscan Media, 2022), 17.

12 Daniel Goleman, "Leadership That Gets Results," *Harvard Business Review*, 2000, https://hbr.org/2000/03/leadership-that-gets-results.

13 Rohr, *Things Hidden*, 22–23.

14 Ibid., 23.

15 Adapted with permission from Rohr, *Things Hidden*, 17.

CHAPTER 8

1   Jenny Gross, "Can You Have More than 150 Friends?" *New York Times*, May 11, 2021, https://www.nytimes.com/2021/05/11/science/dunbars-number-debunked.html.

2   "Dunbar's Number: Why We Can Only Maintain 150 Relationships," BBC, accessed May 26, 2023, https://www.bbc.com/future/article/20191001-dunbars-number-why-we-can-only-maintain-150-relationships.

3   Malcolm Gladwell, *The Tipping Point: How Little Things Can Make a Big Difference* (Boston: Back Bay Books, 2000).

4   Ibid.

5   "Domesday: Britain's Finest Treasure," The National Archives, accessed May 26, 2023, https://www.nationalarchives.gov.uk/domesday/.

6   Maria Konnikova, "The Limits of Friendship," *New Yorker*, October 7, 2014, https://www.newyorker.com/science/maria-konnikova/social-media-affect-math-dunbar-number-friendships.

7   Bruno Goncalves, Nicola Perra, and Alessandro Vespignani, "Modeling Users' Activity on Twitter Networks: Validation of Dunbar's Number," *PLoS One* 6, no. 8 (2011): doi:10.1371/journal.pone.0022656.

8   "Dunbar's Number: Why We Can Only Maintain 150 Relationships," BBC.

9   Nicole B. Ellison, Charles Steinfield, and Cliff Lampe, "Connection Strategies: Social Capital Implications of Facebook-Enabled Communication Practices," *New Media & Society* 13, no. 6 (2011): doi:10.1177/1461444810385389.

10 Christopher McCarty et al., "Comparing Two Methods for Estimating Network Size," *Human Organization* 60, no. 1(2001): 28–39, doi.10.17730/humo.60.1.efx5t9gjtgmga73y.

11 Ibid.

12 Robin Dunbar, "Why Drink Is the Secret to Humanity's Success," *Financial Times*, August 10, 2018, https://www.ft.com/content/c5ce0834-9a64-11e8 -9702-5946bae86e6d.

13 Christopher Roosen, "Dunbar's Number—Relationships Are a Limited Numbers Game," *Christopher Roosen: Adventures in a Designed World* (blog), April 26, 2019, https://www.christopherroosen.com/blog/2019/4/26 /relationships-are-a-limited-numbers-game.

14 Kahlil Gibran, "On Marriage," in *The Prophet* (New York: Alfred A. Knopf, 2018).

15 Solomon E. Asch, "Studies of Independence and Conformity. A Minority of One Against a Unanimous Majority," *Psychological Monographs: General and Applied* 70, no. 9 (1956): 1–70, doi:10.1037/h0093718.

16 Henry Kimsey-House, Karen Kimsey-House, Phillip Sandahl, and Laura Whitworth, *Co-Active Coaching: Changing Business, Transforming Lives* (3rd ed.) (Boston: Nicholas Brealey Publishing, 2011), 33.

17 Ibid.

18 Stephen R. Covey, *The 7 Habits of Highly Effective People: Powerful Lessons in Personal Change* (New York: Free Press, 2004).

19 Kimsey-House et al., *Co-Active Coaching*, 35.

20 Kimsey-House et al., *Co-Active Coaching*, 37.

21 Ibid.

22 The phrase appears in a thirteenth century text that has been translated online by Zara Houshmand, https://iranian.com/Arts/Rumi/1303.html. The text at this website is drawn from this book: *Kolliyaat-e Shams-e Tabrizi*, edited by Badiozzaman Forouzanfar (Tehran, Amir Kabir, 1988).

CHAPTER 9

1 Judith Stein, "Using the Stages of Team Development," MIT Human Resources, accessed May 26, 2023, https://hr.mit.edu/learning-topics/teams /articles/stages-development.

2 Ibid.

3 Denise A. Bonebright, "40 Years of Storming: A Historical Review of Tuckman's Model of Small Group Development," *Human Resource Developmental International* 13, no. 1 (2010): 111–20, doi:10.1080/13678861003589099.

4 Ibid.

5 Model adapted from: Bruce W. Tuckman and Mary Ann C. Jensen, "Stages of Small-Group Development Revisited," *Group & Organization Management* 2, no. 4 (1977): doi:10.1177/105960117700200404.

6 "Is It Safe?" McKinsey Quarterly Five Fifty, accessed May 26, 2023, https:// www.mckinsey.com/featured-insights/leadership/five-fifty-is-it-safe.

7   Amy Edmondson, "Building a Psychologically Safe Workplace | Amy Edmondson | TEDxHGSE," TEDx Talks, May 5, 2014, YouTube video, 11:26, https://youtu.be/LhoLuui9gX8.

8   "Is It Safe?" McKinsey Quarterly Five Fifty.

9   Daniel Pink, *Drive: The Surprising Truth About What Motivates Us* (New York: Riverhead Books, 2009).

10 Mihaly Csikszentmihalyi, *Flow: The Psychology of Optimal Experience* (New York: HarperCollins, 1990).

11 Pink, *Drive*.

12 Carol Dweck, *Mindset: How You Can Fulfill Your Potential* (London: Robinson, 2012).

13 Robert E. Larzelere and Ted L. Huston, "The Dyadic Trust Scale: Toward Understanding Interpersonal Trust in Close Relationships," *Journal of Marriage and Family* 42, no. 3 (1980): 595–604, doi:10.2397/351903.

14 J. David Lewis and Andrew J. Weigert, "Social Atomism, Holism, and Trust," *The Sociological Quarterly* 26, no. 4 (1985): 455–71, https://www.jstor.org/stable/4106098.

15 John K. Rempel, John G. Holmes, and Mark P. Zanna, "Trust in Close Relationships," *Journal of Personality and Social Psychology* 49, no. 1 (1985): 95–112, doi:10.1037/0022-3514.49.1.95.

16 Adapted with Jim McNeish's permission. See Neish website homepage, accessed June 21, 2023, https://neish.co/.

17 Sylvester McNutt (@SylvesterMcNutt), "Closure happens right after you accept that letting go and moving on is more important than projecting a fantasy of how the relationship could've been," Twitter, November 29, 2017, 9:09 PM, https://twitter.com/SylvesterMcNutt/status/936054616600408064.

18 Rick Hanson, *Hardwiring Happiness: The New Brain Science of Contentment, Calm, and Confidence* (New York: Harmony Books, 2013), xxvi.

19 Rick Hanson, "Take in the Good," Rick Hanson, PhD, website, accessed May 26, 2023, https://www.rickhanson.net/take-in-the-good/.

20 "Marriage and Couples," The Gottman Institute, accessed May 26, 2023, https://www.gottman.com/about/research/couples/.

21 Hanson, *Hardwiring Happiness*, xxvi.

CHAPTER 10

1   Don Beck, *Spiral Dynamics Integral*, 2006, Audible audiobook, Chapter 1, 12:46.

2   Beck, *Spiral Dynamics Integral*, Chapter 1, 14:00.

3   Beck, *Spiral Dynamics Integral*, Chapter 1, 15:00.

4   Beck, *Spiral Dynamics Integral*, Chapter 1, 15:26.

5   Don Edward Beck and Christopher Cowan, *Spiral Dynamics: Mastering Values, Leadership and Change* (Hoboken, NJ: Wiley, 2005), 11.

APPENDIX

1   Laurence Freeman et al., *Journey to the Heart: Christian Contemplation through the Centuries*, ed. Kim Nataraja (London: Canterbury Press, 2011), 92; "About Contemplative Practices," Center for Contemplative Mind in Society, accessed May 26, 2023, https://www.contemplativemind.org/practices.

2   Guigo II the Carthusian, *The Ladder of Monks*, trans. Pascale-Dominique Nau (San Sebastian, Spain: Lulu.com, 2013). As referenced in the introduction, this was the context in which Guigo wrote about the four rungs of the "ladder of monks."

3   René Descartes, "*La Recherche de la Vérité par La Lumiere Naturale*" ("The Search for Truth by Natural Light"), 1647, accessed May 26, 2023, https://fr.wikisource.org /wiki/Page:Descartes_-_Œuvres,_éd._Adam_et_Tannery,_X.djvu/535.

4   "Stress Reduction Program," University of Massachusetts Medical School, April 14, 2012, accessed May 26, 2023, https://web.archive.org/web/20120414145938/http://www.umassmed.edu/cfm/stress/index.aspx.

5   Mindful Staff, "Jon Kabat-Zinn: Defining Mindfulness," Mindful, January 11, 2017, https://www.mindful.org/jon-kabat-zinn-defining-mindfulness/.

6   J. Mark Williams, Ian Russell, and Daphne Russell, "Mindfulness-Based Cognitive Therapy: Further Issues in Current Evidence and Future Research," *Journal of Consulting and Clinical Psychology* 76, no. 3 (2008): 524–29, doi:10.1037/0022-006x.76.3.524; Zindel V. Segal, J. Mark G. Williams, and John D. Teasdale, *Mindfulness-Based Cognitive Therapy for Depression: A New Approach to Preventing Relapse* (New York: Guilford Press, 2002).

7   Mindfulness is linked with improved decision-making (C. Marlene Fiol and Edward J. O'Connor, "Waking Up! Mindfulness in the Face of Bandwagons," *The Academy of Management Review* 28, no. 1 (2003): 54–70, doi:10.2307/30040689), divergent thinking (Lorenza S. Colzato, Ayca Ozturk, and Bernhard Hommel, "Meditate to Create: The Impact of Focused-Attention and Open-Monitoring Training on Convergent and Divergent Thinking," *Frontiers in Psychology* 3 (2012): doi:10.3389/fpsyg.2012.00116), and creative problem-solving (Brian D. Ostafin and Kyle T. Kassman, "Stepping out of History: Mindfulness Improves Insight Problem Solving," *Consciousness and Cognition* 21, no. 2 (2012): 1031–36, doi:10.1016/j.concog.2012.02.014); mindfulness can improve employee task performance (Erik Dane, "Paying Attention to Mindfulness and Its Effects on Task Performance in the Workplace," *Journal of Management* 37, no. 4 (2010): 997–1018, doi:10.1177/0149206310367948; Jochen Reb, Jayanth Narayanan, and Sankalp Chaturvedi, "Leading Mindfully: Two Studies on the Influence of Supervisor Trait Mindfulness on Employee Well-Being and Performance," *Mindfulness* 5, no. 1 (2012): 36–45, doi:10.1007/s12671-012-0144-z) and lower turnover intentions (Erik Dane and Bradley J. Brummel,

"Examining Workplace Mindfulness and Its Relations to Job Performance and Turnover Intention," *Human Relations* 67, no. 1 (2014): 105–128, doi:10.1177/0018726713487753).

Experimental studies with US military demonstrate that mindfulness training can generate resilience (Amishi P. Jha et al., "Practice Is Protective: Mindfulness Training Promotes Cognitive Resilience in High-Stress Cohorts," *Mindfulness* 8, no. 1 (2016): 46–58, doi:10.1007/s12671-015-0465-9) and increase individuals' working memory capacity (Amishi P. Jha et al., "Examining the Protective Effects of Mindfulness Training on Working Memory Capacity and Affective Experience," *Emotion* 10, no. 1 (2010): 54–64, doi:10.1037/a0018438).

Mindfulness-based work interventions can lead to higher sales and faster learning (Frank W. Bond, Paul E. Flaxman, and Joda Lloyd, "Mindfulness and Meditation in the Workplace: An Acceptance and Commitment Therapy Approach," *The Psychology of Meditation* (2016): 241–58, doi:10.1093/med:psych/9780199688906.003.0011), and fewer errors in attention processing (Paul A. M. van den Hurk et al., "Greater Efficiency in Attentional Processing Related to Mindfulness Meditation," *Quarterly Journal of Experimental Psychology* 63, no. 6 (2010): 1168–80, doi:10.1080/17470210903249365); mindfulness meditation is linked to higher emotional intelligence (Ornella Tohme and Stephen Joseph, "Authenticity Is Correlated with Mindfulness and Emotional Intelligence," *Journal of Humanistic Psychology* (2020): doi:10.1177/0022167820940926).

Mindfulness-based stress reduction programs can lead to lower burnout and higher well-being for healthcare professionals (Matthew J. Goodman and John B. Schorling, "A Mindfulness Course Decreases Burnout and Improves Well-Being Among Healthcare Providers," *The International Journal of Psychiatry in Medicine* 43, no. 2 (2012): 119–28, doi:10.2190/pm.43.2.b) and their patient encounters (Roberto P. Benzo, Janae L. Kirsch, and Carlie Nelson, "Compassion, Mindfulness, and the Happiness of Healthcare Workers," *EXPLORE* 13, no. 3 (2017): 201–206, doi:10.1016/j.explore.2017.02.001).

8   "What Is Mindfulness?" Mental Health Ireland, accessed February 15, 2023, https://www.mentalhealthireland.ie/mindfulness-evidence-base/.

9   Ibid.

INDEX

ABOUT THE
AUTHOR

Photo by Tom Scott

Patrick Boland is a leadership consultant, executive coach, psychotherapist, and trainer across several industries and sectors around the world. He has worked with organizations ranging from Salesforce to LEGO, Google to Unilever, and Citi to the Center for Action and Contemplation. In 2021, Patrick coauthored a book of reflections, *Every Thing Is Sacred*, with the contemplative teacher Richard Rohr.

In 2013, Patrick founded Conexus, an organization that coaches leaders and their teams using a combination of neuroscience; depth psychology; and embodied, experiential learning. He provides in-person and online leadership programs, team development events, and executive coaching for a wide variety of global organizations. He holds undergraduate and post-graduate degrees in international commerce, Italian, guidance and counselling, education, theological studies, executive and leadership coaching, and psychotherapy. In 2015, he gave a TEDx talk at Trinity College Dublin on the topic of "Failure and the Importance of Mentors."

Patrick lives with his family near Dublin, Ireland, and spends much of his free time sailing or playing football with his son.

The Contemplative Leader
Online Course

Book Patrick for Keynote addresses, Masterclasses, Retreats and Leadership Programs on The Contemplative Leader.

A virtual Masterclass and an in-depth, online Contemplative Leader course (featuring additional content) are available at:

thecontemplativeleader.com

Executive Coaching and Leadership Consulting

Patrick is the Managing Director of *Conexus*, a company that provides Executive Coaching and Leadership Consulting to global clients.

For all inquiries:

conexus.ie

CONEXUS

COACHING LEADERS, CONNECTING TEAMS